Beloved Sister

the letters of
James Henry Gleason

Published works of Duncan and Dorothy Gleason –

Windjammers, an etched book. 1922

Islands of California. 1950

Islands and Ports of California. 1958

Sketches and Paintings from Mexico. 1963

Range Light. 1951-1959
    Publication of Los Angeles Power Squadron

El Noticiero. 1962-1965
    Publication of Los Fiesteros de Los Angeles

Magazine articles, book reviews and special features

JAMES HENRY GLEASON, 1823-1861
Author of these letters
Grandfather of Duncan Gleason

Beloved Sister

the letters of
James Henry Gleason
1841 to 1859

from Alta California
and the Sandwich Islands

with a brief account of his voyage in 1841
via Cape Horn to Oahu and California

compiled with notes by
Duncan and Dorothy Gleason

illustrations by Duncan Gleason
with portraits and facsimiles

THE ARTHUR H. CLARK COMPANY
Glendale, California   1978

089286 2   53146

Copyright ©, 1978, by
THE ARTHUR H. CLARK COMPANY

All rights reserved including the rights to
translate or reproduce this work or parts
thereof in any form or by any media.

LIBRARY OF CONGRESS CATALOG CARD NUMBER 78-059242
ISBN 0-87062-126-2

Dedicated to
ELEANOR DUNCAN GLEASON
Mother of Duncan Gleason
who had the foresight
to recognize the beauty
and historical significance
of these letters

Contents

FOREWORD 13
PREFACE 15
THE LETTERS
   The Voyage Journal and Letters from
      Honolulu, 1841-1845 19
   Letters from Monterey, March to August 1846   89
   Letters from California, September 1846 to
      November 1849 135
   Letters from San Francisco and Monterey,
      December 1849 to 1859 167
APPENDICES
   I Tribute to James Henry Gleason,
      by William Heath Davis 213
   II William Heath Davis, by Duncan Gleason 217
INDEX 219

Illustrations

James Henry Gleason portrait . . .	*frontispiece*
Map of the Voyage to Oahu	18
Frances A. Gleason, the "Beloved Sister"	27
Eleanor Duncan Gleason	28
Captain John Paty	37
The Bark "Don Quixote"	39
The Hawaiian Flag, 1843-1959	49
The Brig "Euphemia"	99
A Page from Captain Paty's Log Book	100
Flags of California, 1825-1846	117
The Old Customhouse at Monterey	119
Governor Alvarado's Home at Monterey	120
James Gleason's Letter of January 28, 1847	137
Deed to Gleason from Sam Brannan	138
James Gleason's Letter of September 30, 1850	179

Foreword

The text of this volume dates back three generations to 1841, when James Henry Gleason wrote these affectionate letters to his sister, Frances Gleason, in Plymouth, Massachusetts, telling her of his experiences in the far away Sandwich Islands and in Alta California.

He was born in Plymouth October 22, 1823, and came to the Sandwich Islands by way of Cape Horn in 1841. In 1845 he sailed to Monterey, Alta California, where he married and lived until his death in 1861. He was County Clerk and Recorder of Monterey County in 1857.

This genial young man made many friends. He was a hunter, swimmer, and horseman of skill in spite of his less than perfect health. When serving as supercargo of the trading bark *Don Quixote,* his duty was to ride along the coast in advance of the ship, so that when the *Don Quixote* put in to port with its cargo, there were buyers on hand.

Gleason's wife, Caterina Demetria Watson, was the daughter of an English father, James Pedro Watson, and a Mexican mother, Mariana Buena Ventura Escamillo. After the death of James Henry Gleason, his widow married into the Gomez family.

In this volume the notes on sailing ships and the days of the windjammers, as well as the historical addenda, have been written by Duncan Gleason who gave much time and study to California's marine history in order to portray those romantic white winged vessels depicted in his paintings.

It is at the urging of many students of history who have read these letters that I have gathered up the loose ends to the best of my ability and am happy to launch this collection of recordings of historical events. It will be a memorial to my husband, Duncan, who with his mother preserved and valued the collection.

Our thanks and appreciation go out to all who have given us assistance, particularly to Nancy Stanford, Anna Marie and Everett Hager, Diane Clinton, Robert Cowan, Thomas S. McNeill, Doctor and Mrs. Clayton Garrison and Mr. and Mrs. Donald Grossman.

1977   DOROTHY GLEASON

Preface

The material contained in these letters of my grandfather, James Henry Gleason should make a valuable contribution to original source sidelights on California history. Depicted with all the buoyant enthusiasm of a young man just entering upon a career in a foreign land, he had a strong bond of affection for his sister Frances in Plymouth, Massachusetts, and he embraced every opportunity to write to her whenever a ship departed from the Sandwich Islands or, later, from Monterey.

This correspondence is written in a beautiful Spenserian handwriting, folded and sealed with wax in such a way as to require no envelope. The paper is well preserved and the ink legible after a period of well over one hundred years of existence. On the lower left hand corner appears the name of the vessel that carried the letter, through the courtesy of the captain, to some port on the Eastern seaboard, where it was either personally delivered or mailed. A postmark served in place of a stamp and the dates indicated that it often took a letter eight months to reach its destination. Some of the pages are written in the regular manner and then turned and inscribed across the page at right angles in a different colored ink, a thrifty Yankee trick to save paper but extremely difficult to read.

Except for a slight extra spacing at the end of sentences, no attempt has been made to correct spelling or punctuation, as the quaint errors give a better picture of a young man of limited schooling suddenly thrown into an environment of culture and trying to overcome his handicap. His naive humor makes even the passages of a personal nature interesting reading. Though his home life in Plymouth had not been happy he held a great desire to see his sister once more. This wish was never fulfilled.

The letters were preserved by an uncle of James Henry, the Reverend Herbert Gleason of Boston, and in 1892 were turned over to my mother, Eleanor Duncan Gleason, who added them to her ever growing collection of documents and articles about the early days of California. The Reverend Herbert, in transmitting the letters, wrote that James Henry was a willful unpredictable boy, always getting into some mischief but afterwards appearing so contrite that he was forgiven.

Here are vivid impressions of an eye witness to a colorful period in the history of the Sandwich (Hawaiian) Islands and of Alta California, portraying the tearing down of the Hawaiian flag and its subsequent raising, the similar lowering and replacement of the Mexican flag in California, a record of the square-rigged sailing ships that plied to and fro from this section of the Pacific to all parts of the world, the final raising of the Stars and Stripes at Monterey, and the frantic days of the California Gold Rush.

The letters of James Henry Gleason end with that of July 20, 1859, likely due to failing strength for he was a frail man in spite of his assertions that he was in good health most of the time. Mr. Gleason died at Monterey in 1861 at the age of 38 years and was buried beneath the pines in the Monterey cemetery.

1950   JOE DUNCAN GLEASON

The Journal and Letters
of
James Henry Gleason

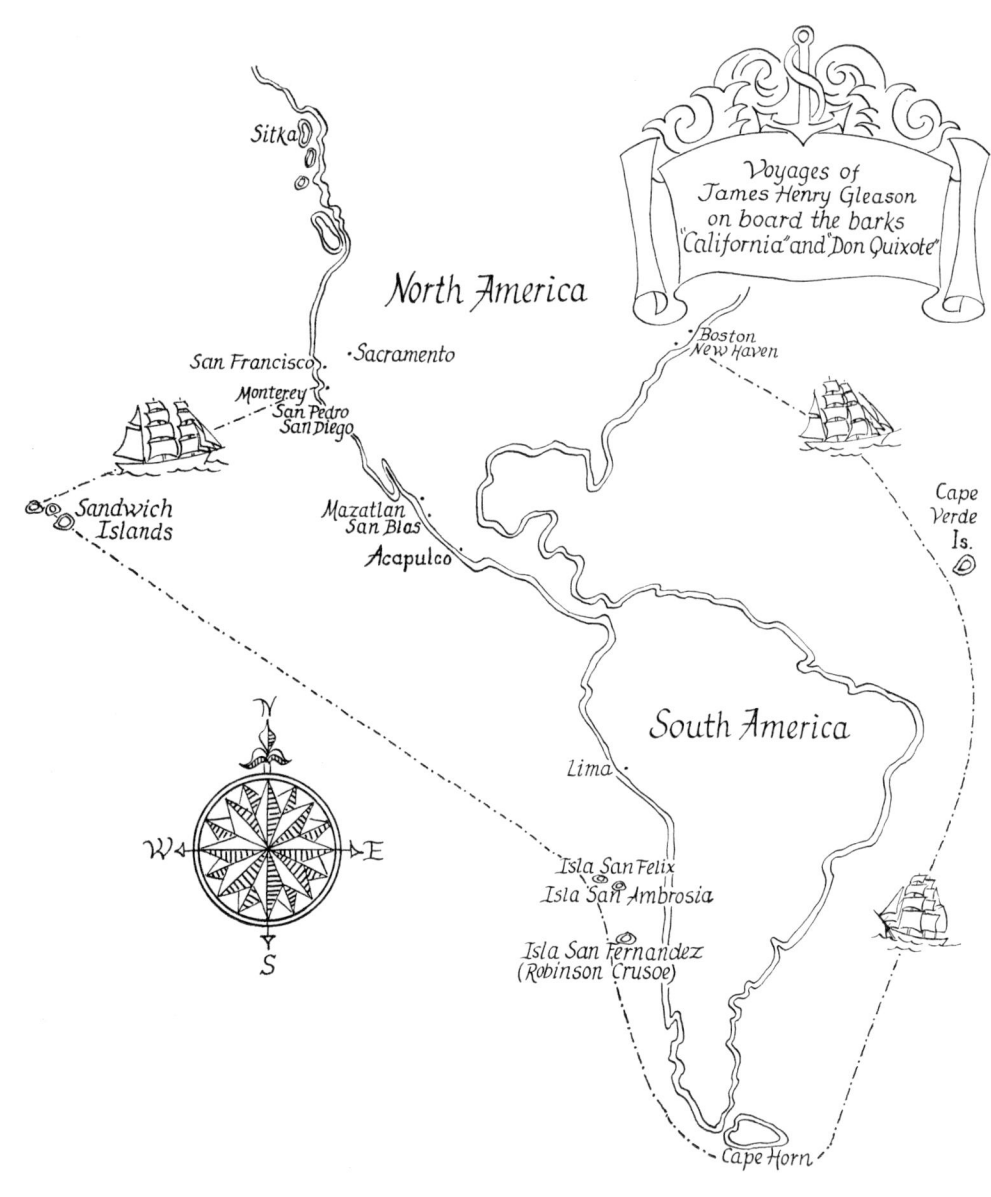

I

The Voyage Journal and Letters from Honolulu, 1841-1845

EXTRACTS FROM A JOURNAL[1] KEPT AT SEA ON BOARD SHIP CALIFORNIA[2] WHILE ON HER PASSAGE FROM BOSTON TO OAHU

We exchanged adieus with our friends, and left the port of Boston with a favourable wind and stood out to sea on our long and dreary passage, the first night out the ship began to roll and tumble about very heavily, and our new beginners began to feel Strong Symptoms of sea sickness, I really pittied them   for once I was blessed with the same disagreeable feeling myself, but however every thing went on very nicely, when we had been at sea a week the boys looked bright and cheerful; and when the topsails were reefed the yards came to the mast head with the tune of "Cheerly men"   my fellow passengers were all strangers to me, but I was not long in making myself acquainted with them, in Wm. D. M. Howard[3] I soon found a friend and companion.

---

[1] This Journal of the voyage was included in a letter to Miss Frances Gleason, November 14, 1842. This portion of that letter is placed here for better chronological sequence.

[2] The ship *California* belonged to the well-known Boston shipping firm of Bryant & Sturgis, pioneers in the California hide trade. (William Heath Davis, *Seventy-five Years in California*. San Francisco, 1929, p. 24). Their fleet included the two vessels made famous by Richard Henry Dana – the brig *Pilgrim* and the ship *Alert*. The *California* sailed from Boston in 1841 carrying James Henry Gleason as far as Oahu, Sandwich Islands.

[3] William D. M. Howard had disturbed the tranquility of his respectable Bostonian family by getting into so much youthful mischief that they shipped him to sea before the mast on the ship *California*. He was bright and active

Our Captain is very pleasant and accommodating, always in high spirits, he allows no cards to be brought into the cabin, but will join with us in our sports and amusements below, singing songs, sky-larking, &c. I shall realise a pleasant time among such agreeable shipmates.

When we had been at sea three weeks we fell in with the Bark "Congo" of Bristol from the coast of Africa Bound to B. a fortnight previous she had been struck with lightning and experienced considerable damage, such as with the loss of her three topmast, fore-mast, jib, & flying-jib-boom, one man was injured by the fall of the topsail sheets but soon recovered. we supplied them with provisions and other necessary articles a boat load of shrowding we received in return.

Aug. 15th. To day we passed the Cape de Verde distant forty miles, if the weather had been clear we should probably had seen them, the next day a Barque hove in sight to the wind ward, at 4 O'c in the afternoon she was near enough for us to speak her. She proved to be the "Rio Packet" of London from Zansabar bound to L. the mate came on board and spent the remainder of the afternoon and took tea with us, this was the first time I ever saw a visit made in the

---

so the captain took compassion on him and ordered him aft to serve as cabin boy, in which capacity he arrived at Monterey early in 1839. At San Pedro he left the ship to enter the employ of Abel Stearns, a prominent merchant of Los Angeles. On his next voyage to Boston aboard the *California* he served as her supercargo or business agent. During the return passage in 1842 he fell in love with a passenger, Mary Warren, and they were married when the ship touched at Honolulu. Howard became very wealthy and took an important part in the building of San Francisco, where a street was named for him. He promoted and was first president of the Society of California Pioneers. The firm of Mellus, Howard & Company donated the first fire engine of the hand pump variety. It was named "Howard." (Davis, *Seventy-five years in California,* pp. 210, 213, 227-28.)

The Voyage Journal

middle of the ocean although it is frequently the case particularly among whalemen.   there was a large package of letters sent home by our passengers among which I sent a Journal, On the evening of the first of Sept we crossed the Equator in Long 17½. the next day we fell in with the trade winds which blew very hard, the trade winds of course favourable to us, and our experienced Capt seemed to take this advantage and "cracked on" and the old ship is now driving on under a heavy press of sail over, and at times through the mountainous billows deluging our decks with water, the royal yards and masts have this day been sent down and and everything lashed securely for rough weather for we are fast approaching Cape Horn.

Aug 19th, we layed too all this day and night under a close reef'd main-topsail and spencers rolling scuppers too.

Oct 5th. To day we made Cape Blanco on the eastern part of Patagonia, this is the first land we have seen since leaving Cape Cod being seventy six days at sea the barren coast and large heaving rocks really seemed pleasant to us while we were sailing by them, and we felt convinced that the dark, deep, and fathomless ocean, that we had been buffeting for months past was not at least shoreless; while we were amusing ourselves looking at that land which was about fifteen miles distant, we were arroused by distant thunder, the Capt ordered the top gall't sails and steering sails to be taken in immediately,   before his orders could be executed the squall struck the ship, all that could be heard amidst the roar of the tempest, was to [hear the Captains strong voice shouting "let go"] [4] everything, the

---
[4] Bracketed text phrases are inserts of probable wording from missing portions of the original letters. Bracketed letter headings are cover addresses of the letters.

topsail haliards fore, and aft, were [let go on the run,] and the yards came down on the caps with a cra[sh – seemingly] to shake every mast to splinters, the top gall't s[heets were] all parted, and the loftly sails high up in the [tem]pest were slapping at their leisure; the fore and [?] fore sail and main sail, were clewed up and furl[ed,] main [top] sail close reefed, a heavy hail storm attending the [tem]pest combined to make it still more fiercer, but our good old and stout ship staggered it out till morning under her close reef topsails when the gale subsided, and all sail was again set, and the ship California is once more away gliding gracefully over the blue waters.

Oct 8th. This morning early we made Staten Land on our weather bow, at six O'c in the evening we passed Cape St Johns distant ten miles   at 8 O'c. the ships course was altered for Cape Horn, it was a splendid sight to look on shore to the mountains, their tops were towering up above the clowds covered with snow, whilst below on the sea shore could be distinctly seen the breakers.   the sun set clear and beautiful, and the heavens around had the appearance of a pleasant night.

Oct 10th. To day we have a fair view of the Cape which is under our lea distant 8 miles, the heaving billows are dashing over its huge rocks and throwing the spray in all directions,

Oct 11th. To day we are driving along under double reef topsails through a heavy snow storm

> That rolls our Barque
> Untill her gunwale kisses the green waves.

Oct 18th. This forenoon a heavy squall struck the ship   before the sails could be taken in several large seas boarded us but did no great damage, the ship was hove too under her close reefed main topsail and laid too till the next day evening, – the weather was very cold occassioned by a southerly wind which blew off the ice.

Oct 20th. This was a very unpleasant day, cold thick and rainy It blew very hard in squalls which I heeded not for I was below amusing myself with a friend; at noon the wind hauled around to the southward, the weather braces were hauled in and the ship is once more driving along with a fair wind, at the rate of nine miles an hour.

> The flowing billows close o'er our path
> Hissing and roaring as if in wrath
> On! On! we dash through foam and spray
> To the Sand'ch Isles we stear our way.

Oct 27th. To day we passed the Island of Juan Fernandes the well known island that Robbinson Crusoe was wrecked upon.

Oct 30th. To day we passed the Felix and Ambrose Islands on the weather bow, the royal masts were sent up fore and aft to day, and preparations made for pleasant weather,

Nov 20th [? 6th]. This was a pleasant day.   in the forenoon the boats were taken away from the quarter deck and lashed alongside of the launch which made a good promenade for us to walk, sometimes for two long hours after tea. In the afternoon (this being Saturday) the Capt ordered the crew to put away their work and wash the decks down clean for Sunday. This being accomplished they began to muster around the forecastle rejoicing to think that they were to have the remainder of the afternoon to their amusements but they had not much time for reflection before the second mate called them aft to get some old sails up from below to mend. This unexpected demand caused them to change their pleasing countenances and don a sulky face, they however knew that such orders must be obeyed, consequently they went about their work with vigor. at 4 o'c the second steward, cook, crew, &c mustered around the after hatchway to receive their allowance of water as the carpenter served it up to them, in most vessels where the crew are put on an allowance, the third mate serves it out but in our situation where we had none, the carpenter was appointed to act as one in this case which pleased him very much to think that he was capable of holding such an office.

Nov 13th. To day at 10 A.M. we spoke the whaleship "L. C. Richmond" nine months out with fifty barrels of oil.

Nov 16th. To day we crossed the equator in the Pacific Ocean in Long 116½, we have for the last few days had pleasant weather.

Nov 24th. Preparations were made to day for the coming of Thanksgiving, fresh pork prepared, pies and wine got up from below &c, and tomorrow is the day for the celebration.

Nov 25th. To day in America is a day of humiliation and prayer but not so with us, we have a good dinner and a fair wind which was something uncommon with us but was no more than we fully realized.

Dec 1st. This forenoon the anchors were got off the bow, chains bent, hausers got up from below &c, for we are fast approaching the land, We passed Owyhee early in the morning and made the Island of Mowe at noon, we kept the land in sight the remainder of the day. in the evening at 7 O'c the Capt gave orders to take in all sails but the three topsails, and a strict

The Voyage Journal 25

watch to be kept during the night, for we expect to see Oahu before daylight.

Dec 2nd. This day ends the trials, and wanderings of our long and dreary passage, Oahu is now before us in all its fragrant beauty   thou are the

> "Isles of the ocean! Lion of the Seas!
>   Child of the waves! and nursling of the breese!
> Thou sittest proudly on thy ocean throne,
>   A sceptered queen, majestic, not alone,
> Above the gentlest airs in gladness meet,
>   And billows break in music at thy feet."

9 o'c A.M. Our sails are furled, the voyage is over. 10 o'c A.M. I'm now in the boat to be rowed on shore.

The Letters

[cover: Miss Frances Gleason
        Plymouth, Mass, U.S.A.]

Oahu   Dec 6th 1841

Dear Sister

I arrived here on the 2d inst in good health after a pleasant passage of 154 days. I found the Sandwich islands much more pleasant than I expected to. Tis now mid winter and very warm, trees, flowers, &c in bloom   everything has a gay and brilliant appearance. It was a splendid sight on comming in the harbor

In the morning at daylight we made the island of Oahu directly ahead, the mountain tops were towering up above the clouds which looked dismal whilst below in the valleys waved the tall green grass   now & then large feilds of Cocoa and Bananas trees could be seen towering to the skies and their large leaves waving too and fro in the sweet scented breeze. At nine oc we passed Diamond hill and then opened to my view that longed looked for village Oahu   At ten oc we took a Pilot and came to anchor outside the reef distant two miles from the town

> "Our sails are furled the voyage is o'er
> And I'm now in the boat to be rowed on shore
> The heavens above wore a pleasant smile
> When our Barque was moored by that fairy isle."

We'll change the scene
Picture to your imagination a large room elegantly furnished   on the wall hangs in large mahogany frames the following pictures Bark Don Quixote laying at anchor in Oahu harbour, Schooner Moss sailing along the land, Westminster hall and Abbey, &c   in the middle of the room stand a large centre table   on a tall statue rested a large lamp which throwed its brilliant light over books of all descriptions which lay scattered about upon the table   Their sat a young man of 18 just entered manhood his coat thrown aside vest unbottoned collar thrown back o'er his shourlders in his right hand he holds a pen with his arm lay resting on the table and he had thrown himself in that attitude which persons frequently do when they are in deep thought probably thinking of something important to write in the sheet before him.

The person above described is Frances if you have not guessed is your brother James writing a letter home to his sister. The vessel will sail tomorrow-morning that is to convey this letter to America theirfore I have taken this opportunity 12 oc at night to conclude it   I trust the next letter that you receive it will be longer and written better [I shall] expect a long answer in return for this, Adieu!

Send my love to all [   ]   Mary ann Martha ann

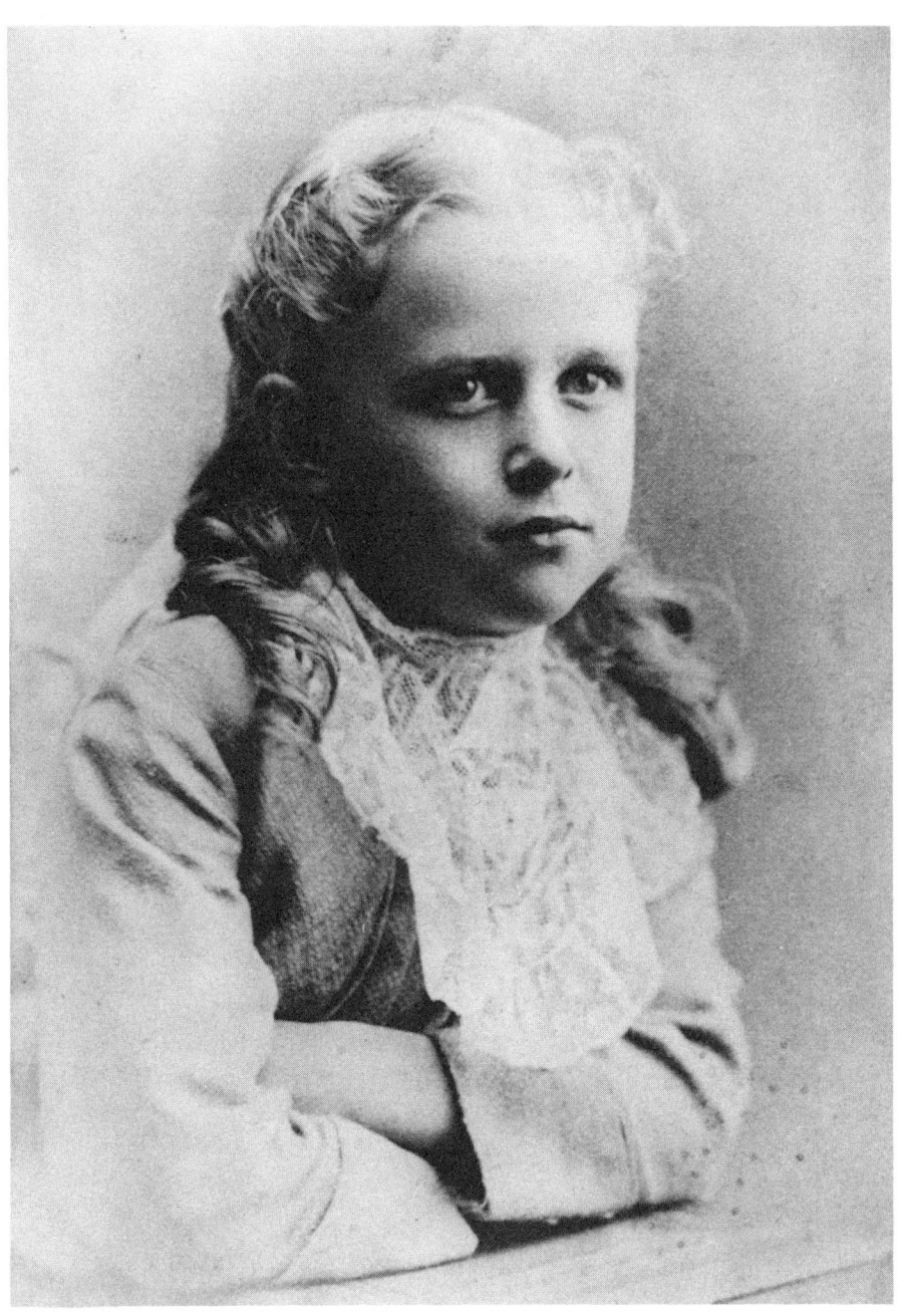

FRANCES A. GLEASON AS A CHILD
Beloved Sister of James Henry Gleason

Eleanor Duncan Gleason
The mother of Duncan Gleason, whose interest aided in the preservation of these letters. This book is dedicated to her.

William[5] also send their love to all enquiring friends. This Dear Frances   from Your Affectionate Brother
James

[cover: Miss Frances A. Gleason
            Plymouth, Mass, U.S.America
Ship Glouchester, Capt Easterbrooks
(Arrived Waring, Mass., June 27 – Postage 12)]

Honolulu   Jan 10th 1842

Dear Sister,

I am at present acting as salesman in the store with Uncle William and enjoying very good health   I like my situation very well and in a short time I am in hopes to understand the native language.

Uncle John [Paty] is on the coast of California and enjoying very good health and prospects of making a good voyage   he has perfectly recovered his health from his sickness on board the Barque while on her passage from Valparaizo to this port; our dear Uncle Henry, can what I hear be true, must it be that he is no more that good, kind, and affectionate unkle. Alas our Grandmother I send my warmest and tenderest sym-

---

[5] Mary Ann was Mrs. John Paty, and Martha Ann was Mrs. William Paty. William and John Paty were uncles of James Henry Gleason, welcoming him into their home and giving him a clerkship in their mercantile business. The Sandwich Islands at that time were the center of the seafaring world, the crossroads of trade to the Orient, the islands of the Pacific and the coast of California. The two Captains Paty were important personages of this kingdom. William served as harbormaster of the port of Honolulu in 1842 and actively engaged in the business of freight and passenger service. Captain John was considered one of the ablest navigators on the Pacific Ocean. In 1846 the Hawaiian king made him his "Commodore" with a dress uniform and the privilege of flying the nation's flag from his vessels, virtually serving as His Majesty's representative in foreign affairs. (Honolulu, Hawaii Public Archives, History Shelf, 1842-43; Davis, *Seventy-five Years in California*, pp. 109, 188, 191-94, 254.)

pathies to her, and Henry's sisters; our Aunts. I understand by Uncle William that he died very happily after an illness of 8 days and was then freed from a world of troubles. He was much respected here and is greatly missed among this small community & by his Brothers he was their almost daily companion

 Sister we have dear friends yes those to whom we cannot with words express our gratitude Uncle William's first enquires were on my arrival if you or my brothers were ill-used by our present mother, what had I to reply? I could not have him know that you were ill-used neither could I say with a clear concience that you were used well, therefore I made a few brief and encouraging remarks in reply to his question. Try to comfort yourself and our younger Brothers are the words that I shall have to conclude this short letter with as business is very brisk with us at present & this will be the only letter I shall write by this conveyance. I have finished one to George White that I commenced three weeks sail from home and continued it as a journal. I now bid Adieu by sending my love to all enquiring friends tell them to write often and not wait a chance of answering my letters but give me a chance of answering theirs.

Ever your true & sincere Brother
James H. Gleason

[pr "Delaware" – postage 12]

Honolulu Oahu Sand'ch Isl'ds
Feb'y 22d 1842

My Dear Sister

 I avail myself of this opp'y now offered pr Brig "Chacabuca" to write to you all the important and entertaining news now circulating in this little world of *Sunshine* and Garden of *Paradise* and likewise to inform you of the good health and happiness prevailing among the Paty Generation residing at Honolulu S. I. We are looking for letters from home daily and even hourly hoping they will be as lengthy written as I have been anticipating their arrival   Tell Grand'r that we received letters from Uncle John on the 11th inst acquainting us with the favourable prospects of making a good voyage   he will return in the Spring with a full Cargo consisting principally of Hides and Asst Lumber and [will] fill up with other goods that he can make most available in this [and] the Valp'o markets   he thinks of taking Mary Ann and Coz Johnny with him next voyage which will make considerable deduction in our large family circle   I shall regret Johnny absense very much for he affords me good amusement   I wish you could see the little Jewel *Nelly Blue* (Hellen D. Paty)⁶ to make my letter *Short* & *Sweet* I shall describe her in one word that she is a "Wonder" and sends her love to you in the shape of a cake with *'lasses* in it to make it sweet   She thinks of calling on you when she comes that way to make a long visit so be prepared   I have not realized any fears of home–sickness nor yet expect to so long as I have such beauties to attract my attention and such good friends as I now have to guide and direct my youthful days but however I anticipate strong hopes of coming home and be a good boy as soon as I have cut my cake   I have offered Mary Ann a spare page in this letter to write to you but she will not accept of it and is not going to write untill she receives a line from you to answer there to   she writes with me in send-

---
⁶ John and Nelly Blue were children of Captain John Paty.

ing love to all who own a name or relationship to the Paty's and to all who feel an interest in thier welfare but I am fast coming to a conclusion and before I conclude I must state how happy I should be if I were at home to day to join with you (as Mary Ann joins with me) in celebrating the Birthday of the great renowned Patriot "Washington"   I must now close or I shall get my letter to an unusual length. Please present my best respects to Friend George.
   Your Affectionate Brother J. H. Gleason

Honolulu Oahu S. I.
March 4th 10 oc A.M.   Dear Sister   I have unfolded and resumed the pen that is to trace the lines in the most important part of my letter to inform you that the long looked for arrival is at hand   William has this moment (11 A.M.) handed me a letter from my Dear Sister Dated Oct 11/41   I perused its long and interesting contents till I have got it thoroughly by heart I hope that all letters that succeed it will be its equal as regard to length and good news   how happily pleased I am to hear that

> Times aint now as they used to was,
> Can't buy *Rum* as you used to could,

And thousand other sentences similar which I shall have to omit for want of leasure to compose.

 George White's dated Oct 10/41 is now before me,
 Coz Caroline's and Edward's dated ————————
I expect is on the way.

 G. W. informs me that Caroline had a party on her birthday evening and no "Gentlemen" were invited "What a shame."

 Also informs me that F———y has caught a Beau "I shant tell you who 'tis"   You see that I have con-

trived by short *sentences, blanks, corners, crooks,* and *turns,* to get my letter to a tolerable good length   I have come to one termination and am fast coming to the second   The letters written by this conveyence will probably be detained in Valp'o some time therefore I have not written but this one letter by this opp'y to the U. States   I shall write to Father by next opp'y   tell him to write often and likewise *all* who feel interested, thus with an Adieu! I close the Epistle.
   Your Affc't Brother J. H. Gleason

Since writing the foregoing I have learned that [the] Brig "Delaware" returns again to the U. States in a short time consequently I shall fill out the remaining lines and send it by the Delaware. I hope and presume to say that you'll find this letter interesting notwithstanding its old date and curious construction but "Circumstances alter cases" (as the old saying is) and I sincerely hope that the interest and pleasure you'll take while perusing its long contents will be no way impaired by its simple construction and olden date   I have nothing further to add Remember me to Caroline, Edward, Aunt and Uncle Cooper   tell them to write often and also write to
  Your Affectionate Brother James H. Gleason
     by every opportunity, Adieu!
       J.H.G. J.H.G.

[pr Whaleship "Briganza"]
    Honolulu Oahu Sandch Islands
            Sept 20th '42
To Miss Frances A. Gleason, Plymouth
My Dear Sister
 I improve an opportunity offered pr Whaleship

"Briganza" bound for New Bedford to inscribe a few lines to you which will inform you of my good health and that of our relations here.

I had quite an ill-turn a few months ago occasioned by the climate and was confined to the house for nearly four weeks. You will be gratified to learn that I received all the kindness and attention from Cousin Martha Ann [Mrs. William Paty] during my sickness that one could wish   we moved into the Valley and by experiencing a change of air I soon recovered my health.

The Valley is a place where the foreign residents retire to in the heat of the season, you are there favoured with the good cool and refreshing breese from the mountains which together with being freed from the dust of the village makes it extremely pleasant and agreeable. Uncle William has built him a new house there this season and christened it "Strawberry Cottage" which name it still retains. it is built of straw with a veranda all around the building shaded with vines in front   it is a beautifull place without comparison, 'twould make you laugh to see it. Nelly Blue is more interesting than ever and evidently grows handsomer every day   She talks native a good deal and English some. She says "Morning Kemo" very distinctly so you see I am honored with a new name.

The "Don Quixote"[7] arrived here on the 12th of May last quite unexpectedly as Uncle William had then given up the idea of her coming down this season. She returned on the 31th making a short stay of about

---

[7] The bark *Don Quixote* was a favorite in the packet and freight trade up and down the western coast of the Americas and made trips from Massachusetts to the Sandwich Islands. She was one of the vessels owned by Captains William and John Paty and is mentioned thirty-nine times in Bancroft's *History of California*.

three weeks. Aunt Mary Ann & John Henry took passage in her   She will return here again by the middle or last of Dec'r next,

We are looking daily with all the anxiety *possible* for the arrival of the "Victoria" & "Sarah Abigail" from the U. States   the former has been out from N. York over six months and had ought to have been here a forghtnight ago   I anticipate lots of letters from yourself, as long, as long, as long as a — — — — — — — — Railroad.

21st 8 Oc A.M.

Sail O, has just been cried by at least a hundred voices, the "Sarah & Abagil" is at hand   I am too impatient to write more at present merely to say that Uncle William has just gone out to her, in company with Capt Brewer and several others. *more anon*

22d 4 Oc P.M.

I have just been able to obtain the letters as they were stowed away down in the hold of the vessel   the Brig sails early in the morning consequently I shall have to write all I have in view this evening   I regret very much that I could not have got them before so as to have written you a long letter but as tis here goes (not till after supper though for those letters that I have just been reading have given me an enormous appetite particularly G. Whites)   there is yet a package on board which has not yet been received and I fear that we shall not be able to obtain it before I close this although I shall leave it unclosed till the last moment but first let me acknowledge the receipt of this handfull that I have by me vis one from G. White I. T. Hall and Cos Caroline and two from yourself all of which I am very much pleased with and will answer them all by the earliest opportunity which will be by the Sarah & Abagil or Jos Peabody   they both sail in about four months for the States   you must make my appoligies to them for not writing by this conveyance   I expect they will be disappointed but tell them to commit themselves to the future with a courrageous and unfaltering hope that they will sh[ ] come to hand   I called at Mrs Brewers last evening and [had] the infinate pleasure of seeing Mrs Nye[8] it seeme[d] pleasant to hold converse with a person direct from my own loved home (although not on very amicably terms) those little items of news that one would hardly think of communicating would be quite enouge to produce an excitement in the mind of any person that has been long absent.

Enclosed you will find a letter for your own private reading in which I have communicated all that is interesting to you, let no one see it for the world. I was very much pleased with yours.

I must soon bring this to a close for I'm getting tired and sleepy. Good Night.

Your Affectionate Brother
James

Remember me to all my friends

[Miss Frances A. Gleason & Mr. James H. Gleason]
PRIVATE CORRESPONDENCE   Dear Beloved Sister, Picture yourself your far distant brother flourishing in a foreign clime with good prospects before him and a sincere determination to visit again his own loved home the place of his birth and childhood   you are to be envied my Dear Sister in being so fortunate as to choose

---

[8] Mrs. Nye was the wife of Captain Nye of the American brig *Bolivar*.

CAPTAIN JOHN PATY, 1837-1868
James Henry Gleason's uncle who captained many vessels
in both California waters and on the long trip from
Massachusetts around Cape Horn to the Sandwich Islands
and Pacific ports. Respected and admired, he was
considered one of the best navigators of his day.
Courtesy of The Public Archives, Honolulu

THE BARK "DON QUIXOTE", FROM A PAINTING BY DUNCAN GLEASON
On this ship James Henry Gleason served as supercargo for his uncle
Captain John Paty. The ship flew the flag of the Hawaiian Islands
since Captain Paty had been appointed emissary of King Kamehameha IV.

from among the many *buds* a *rose* to be the partner of your affections that your brother so highly esteems I have always had an internal feeling towards A—— T—— but good opportunities have never offered to be very familiar with each other while he was classmate with me   I looked upon him as a person possessed of those qualities which make men *good*   his only aim was study   would that I had improved my time as he did but I was two eager for play, I now begin to feel for the want of that education which I threw away   the society that I am introduced into here hold high stations in life guided wholly by the laws of Etiquete   a person unacquainted with these and without a refined education and graceful in their manners is considered unfit for their company   I have endeavored to elevate myself to that degree which in Plymouth would be termed "top-not"   It seemed odd to me when I first arrived here being always used to hand labour and then suddenly introduced into high society where I had half a dozen servants under me to command not even to put my hand to any thing but it would seem still more odd to me to go home now and split wood & bring water &c   I must bring this to a close for it is growing late and I am getting tired if the vessel does not go in the morning I will write a line to Augustus. I think his name is Augustus M.

I am my dear Sister your very Affectionate Brother
James.

Additionable – P. S. Dont you think that I have improved in writing?   *Say Yes*   Dont for the world let any one see this after you have read it   put a seal on it as big as dollar and if any one goes to it tell them *Taboo loa. 'aole pono.* that's Kanaka

42 *Beloved Sister*

Honolulu Oahu Sand'ch Isld's
Nov'r 14th 1842

To Miss Frances A. Gleason, Plymouth
My Dear Sister

Enclosed in the foregoing pages you will find a Journal of my passage out on board Ship "California"[9] I have sent you this as I have no time to write you a letter for Uncle William has been unwell for the last few days, and I am alone in the store and very busy.

The Ship "Victoria" sails direct for N.Y. on the first of next month by which vessel I shall write home by, as it will be a much better opportunity of writing, and I hope by then that the "Wm Grey" will arrive, that I may answer the letters received by her   She is expected daily.

Uncle William is much better to day   he has been out and down to the store.

I hope you will excuse the brevety of this and remember me to all my Plymouth friends and relations, and all who make enquires after,

Your Affectionate Brother
James

[pr "Chenamus"]

Honolulu   Oahu   Sand'ch Isld's
Nov 20th 1842 [10]

To Miss Frances A Gleason,   Plymouth
My Dear Sister

I embrace with much pleasure this opportunity which offers pr "Chenamus" to write home.   the "Chenamus" is as square as a Sugar Box in her bows,

---

[9] The Journal is that which appears at the beginning of this chapter.

[10] This letter was written November 20, 1842, and was postmarked received in "Boston, May 11, 1843," a total of 172 days!

and is a very dull sailer, she had a *quick* passage of *One hundred and eighty days* coming out, and will in all probability have a corresponding one going home, if so, it would not be much of an object to write to any length by the opportunity. The "Wm Grey" has been here four days, and I have not as yet got one single letter from home. Uncle William and Martha Ann have both got letters from Plymouth, and I cannot think even for a moment that there is none for me, there must be, and I shall be labouring under an expectation of some till the last piece of her cargo is discharged.

I should like to get a Journal from you kept daily, communicate every little item, and incident, no matter how trifling, for it would be of more interest to me out here than you can really imagine   you dont know how much value I set on your letters when received, if you did, you would not fail to send me by every opportunity that offered, a package about 7 by 9 and two inches thick, crowded full of reading matter. I cannot help thinking about you at home now enjoying the pleasures of cold North Easters, (it makes me shiver all over to think of them,) while I am suffering under the effects of a burning sun, dust and musqueters. I would not mind being with you though for a day or two, just for a change. I have just bought ten large Oranges for 12½¢, I wish I could send them to you they look so nice, and sweet, just picked from the trees, I would gladly (if I could) exchange a basket full of them for a good large *home Greening,* or a pint of *Huckleberries.*   green figs and milk, I indulge in the most here   we have them in abundance   you cannot form any kind of an idea how sweet, how delicious. I am not backward at all in the larg Pine Apples, that grow here, yours at home are not to be

compared with them, but the sweetest thing we have on the island to my estimation, is Nelly Blue, a kiss from her which I get every time I go up to the house (I have to hire it sometimes though) is better, far better, than anything you can imagine in the fruit line. She is certainly the finest little beauty you ever saw, her father and mother have been talking strongly lately of packing her up in a box and sending her home. She is down to the store this afternoon with me, and "bothers" me so that I cannot write any more at present.
More Anon.

Nov 23d 1842 Wednesday

The "Chenamus" sails in a few hours, so I must write hastily. I have waited till the last moment for finishing my letter, that I might have a chance of acknowledging the receipt of some letters from home per "Wm Gray" but I have not received any yet, but I cannot believe but what there must be some on board stowed away.

We have [had] some very interesting news here lately, which you have probably heard of at home ere this, that the Ameri[cans] took possession of the Coast of California and gave it up again in a few days.[11] The

---

[11] Under command of Commodore Thomas ap Catesby Jones, the Pacific Squadron was lying at Callao, Peru, in August of 1842, with the frigate flagship *United States* and the sloop-of-war *Cyane*. A British squadron lay in the harbor and, as war with Mexico was imminent, the Commodore watched the movements of the British closely, since they might attempt to take possession of California in the event of war being declared. At a ball on board *H.M.S. Vanguard,* the American officers overheard that the ship was to sail the following morning, consequently Commodore Jones slipped out of the harbor at daybreak with all sail set for Monterey.

Arriving off Monterey, they saw the Mexican trading bark *Jóven Guipuzcoana* leaving port, but a shot across her bow brought her into the wind. Putting aboard a boat's crew, she was ordered back to Monterey. Don José Joaquin Estudillo was a passenger on the bark with his young daughter, María de Jesús, who later became the wife of William Heath Davis.

Commodore Jones hastened to demand the surrender of the town. Governor Alvarado had left for his rancho, leaving instructions however, for Commandante Captain Mariana Silva to surrender the town, which was formally done. Thomas O. Larkin, later United States consul, received news from Mexico that war had not been declared, so the flag was hauled down and California returned to Mexican rule. The *Jóven Guipuzcoana* was released and the whole affair celebrated with a ball at the home of Mr. Larkin at which Captain John Paty and William Heath Davis were guests.

The *Don Quixote* had arrived in Monterey and Captain Paty's wife was on board. She is described as being very intellectual and a witty conversationalist, a favorite at the parties and dances given aboard the flagship. She is said to be the third American lady to come to California, Mrs. Larkin and Mrs. Spear having preceded her.

Captain Armstrong of the flagship was fond of waltzing, as was Captain Paty. The one was very large and the other small and wiry. An endurance contest was arranged between them, the ladies seemed to be tireless but the big captain finally gave out and Captain Paty was acclaimed the victor.

When the *United States* returned to Monterey from Hawaii, she again became the flagship and the squadron dropped down the coast to pay respects at Los Angeles to the newly appointed governor, Manuel Micheltorena. Commodore Jones was received most cordially and a banquet followed by a grand ball was provided as entertainment for the recent conquerors. The thrifty Micheltorena however, requested that as reparation for his wounded feelings, the Commodore should give him fifty uniforms for the governor's tattered army, a set of band instruments and $15,000.00 cash. This request the Commodore said he would refer to his government.

The Americans were also entertained at the home of Don Luis Vignes, who had come to California in 1831 from Boston, on the bark *Louisa.* Don Luis located in Los Angeles and planted immense vineyards. He was also a pioneer in the growing of oranges. He presented Commodore Jones with several barrels of choice wine. A street in Los Angeles has been named for Vignes.

With a parting salute to the Mexican flag at San Pedro, the fleet left for Callao. Learning that he was to be relieved of his command by Commodore Dallas, who was coming out in the frigate *Congress,* and wishing to finish his cruise which was to have consumed three years and was only half completed, Commodore Jones set off on a hide and seek game encompassing most of the islands of the Pacific. With the *Congress* following from place to place but never catching up, he took the old "battle-wagon" back to the Atlantic and home. In an investigation of his rash act in taking possession of California, he was exonerated, praised for his vigilance and presented with a gold hilted sword. (Davis, *Seventy-five Years in California,* pp. 111-15, 117, 119-20, 193, 196.)

Thomas Oliver Larkin came to California on the *Newcastle,* arriving in April of 1832. A fellow passenger was Rachel Holmes, traveling out to be with her husband Captain John Holmes. Upon arrival she found that the Captain had died, and in due time married Larkin at Santa Barbara on board the trading vessel *Volunteer.* She was the first American woman to make her home in California. Larkin was captured by the Californians in 1846 and held prisoner as a hostage until the end of the war. He acted as American consul from 1843 until the American occupation, and built the third section of the customhouse at Monterey. A street in San Francisco is named for him.

French have got possession of the Society Islands. I shall write to you next by the "Wm. Gray" she sails in about a month, or six weeks, I should not be surprised if she arrived before you receive this. Give my love to Father, Grandmother, Sylvia, Aunt & Uncle Cooper, Caroline, Edward and all who yet remember me.

Ever Your Affectionate Brother
James.

Additionable, We had a salt fish dinner yesterday it strongly reminded me of home, I had almost forgotten how to eat it, *I soon found out though.*

[pr "George"   Capt Cash]

Honolulu Oahu Sandwich Islands
December 8th 1842 [12]

To Miss Frances A. Gleason, Plymouth
My Dear Sister.

I embrace this opportunity to inform you of my good health, hoping this may find you enjoying that good, and best blessing.

My last to you was under date Novr 20/42, by Brig "Chenamus"   Since then, nothing has transpired worthy of communicating, "nothing but every day scenes of common life"   I go to dancing school twice a week now, I've got to be quite a pretty little dancer, you hav'nt no idea. (so every body says. I dont know anything about it.)   all I wish is that I could be with you on the 22d of this month, to enjoy the pleasures of the evening, and night at the Pilgrim Hall, tell A—— M. T——e to dance a "Cotillion" for me the next set.   by the way, tender my best love to him.

---

[12] This letter was postmarked "New Bedford, May 4, 1843," 148 days en route.

I have just been congratulating myself on my pleasant dream last night, which was, that I received lots of letters from home by the "Wm Gray" I sincerely hope that I did not take the trouble to dream it to no purpose, but vain fancies, and idle dreams, will at times pry themselves on a persons mind, which he realises them no other than true when lost in unconscious sleep, "tired natures sweet restorer."

I was really disappointed though in not getting a line or two from you by the "Wm Gray" you must have missed the opportunity of forwarding them. I shall look forward though to the arrival of the "Delaware" she will be here about the first of March next, when I shall expect lots of letters from you.

The "Chenamus" sailed last Sunday, a salute of thirty six guns was fired by vessels in the harbour to cheer her on her long passage. It considerably broke the monotony of a Sunday morning *that I so much dread*

The U.S. Frigate United States arrived here a few days ago from the Coast of Calif'a. She sails in about an hour I expect there will be quite a display exchanging salutes with the fort soon.

Ned S-e-s-n a particular friend of mine is close by me humming over that pathetick air "Old Zip Coon" and that charming little ballad "Rose of Allendale" very much to his own personal gratification, certainly not to mine for he bothers me so that I shall have to "wind up" hoping you will excuse this brief letter.

Remember me to all my friends and acquaintances at *Home,* tender my respects to Mrs. Sylvester and her family I should be happy indeed to receive a line from them.

Ever Dear Sister, Your Affectionate Brother
James.

[pr "Wm Gray"   Capt Stickney]
Honolulu Oahu S. I.
Feb 28th 1843

To Miss Frances A. Gleason, Plymouth
My dear Sister

The "Wm Gray" bound for the U. States, offers me another opportunity with much pleasure to write home, you will be pleased to hear, that I am blessed with an almost uninturupted health, and I sincerely hope you are enjoying that good and best blessing. The Don Quixote is expected every day from the Coast, and as I shall probably be very busy while she is here, I must commence my letter under this date.

You say in your last letter that you hope I shall not like staying out here so well as at home, 'tis true, I prefer home to any other place, but still it is right that I should remain here, for by so doing, I anticipate good future prospects. I've not yet forgotten those "good old times" at home, those Holiday evenings spent among you at M.– B.–'s E.– H.–'s Cousin C–&c &c.

> "Scenes forever dear,
>   Remembrance hails you with her warmest tear."

I hope you are ambitious, I cannot say that I am, but still I believe I have more ambition than I would have had if I had remained at home, for on coming out here I find that there is more that I can associate with of any respectability, but those that are older, and far better educated than myself. So a strong and ardent desire to become their equals   I devote every leisure moment to books for instruction. My wish is dear Sister that you should strive hard for an education for if you should be involved in any difficulties or wronged any way in after life, how pleasant, and agreeable, it would

THE HAWAIIAN FLAG, 1843-1959

The eight stripes represented the major islands of the group. The British Union Jack was included in consideration for Capt. Vancouver who gave the islands their first flag when King Kamehameha placed his kingdom under the protection of Great Britain, a cession never ratified by Britain. After the 1893 Hawaiian revolution the old flag was retained, and upon annexation to the United States in 1898 was retained as the Territorial flag

be to you, to possess knowledge capable of showing proper resentment to a wrong-doer.

I heard quite a compliment payed you the other day by Cousin M.– She said that you looked just like her Nelly Blue, now N.– B.– is surpassingly lovely, she appears to our eyes the verisimilitude of one of those celestial messengers called angels. Speaking seriously though, you looked beautiful indeed to my eyes, with those ringlets "Curling down your neck so bare" but now since you have got them "done up" behind you must be

"More than painting can express"

But this is not all I have to jud[g]e by, the following quotation from G. W–'s last letter has given me sufficient satisfaction and evidence to the truth of it. "You cannot imagine Jimmy how handsome she has grown she is a perfect beauty without *paint,* or *whitewash"* but this is pushing sweet sounding nonsense to extremes, let us commence on more soberlike realities.

As we are just getting over a little of the excitement that has universally prevailed here for the past fortnight, I must refer to my *journal* and give you some of the particulars.

Saturday Feb 18th 1843

War! War! war! This has been one of the most remarkable days I ever witnessed in my life, in the morning the following notices were posted up in the principal streets of the village.

"To all Americans resident at Honolulu.
"I am requested by Capt I. C. Long of the U.S. Ship "Boston" to
"give publicity to the following letter received last evening.
"H. B. M. Ship "Carysfort" Oahu Feb 17/43
" 'Sir, – I have the honor to notify to you, that H. B. M. Ship
"Carysfort" under my command, will be prepared to make

"an immediate attack upon this town at 4 P.M. tomorrow
"(Saturday) in the event of the demand now forwarded by
"me to the King of these Islands, not being complied with by that
"time. 　　　　　　　　　I have the honor to be &c. &c.
　　　　　　　　　　Signed George T. Paulet, Captain,

"To the Commanders of American vessels in the Port of Honolulu,
"Gentlemen, – I have to request that you will cause all of the boats be-
"longing to your respective ships, to be manned, and sent to R. wharf
"to render any assistance which may be required by Citizens of
"the United States resident here, pending the difficulties between
"this Govt and that of Great Britain and oblige.
　　　　　　　　　　　Yr's &c &c &c Wm Hooper
　　　　　　　　　　　Acting U. S. Com Agent."
"Office of the U. S. Agency
　Oahu S. I. Feb'y 18/43

It was thought universally that the King would sooner see the village laid in a burning mass of ruins, than to comply with the unjust demands of Lord P.–　the people were so confident that hostilities would be made, that they took active, and decided steps, for embarking, waggons, and trucks, loaded down with baggage, was continually passing by down to the wharfs to be put on board of vessels in the harbour, the English Brig "Julia" received on board all of the English ladies in the place, and weighed anchor and stood outside the harbour. Hundreds of natives running into the mountains, with bundles under their arms, others more coureageous, rushing down to the King, determined to stand by him till the last moment, all conspired to make it look indeed warlike. It was decided upon by the Americans, that the ladies should embark at 2 O.c. I was engaged during the forenoon packing up my most valuable articles of clothing, intending to put it on board of the "Wm Gray" and then go up to the house and remain there with Uncle W.— as long as I could get a foothold. At O.c. [*sic*] much to the surprise and astonishment of all, it was brought to an amicable adjustment, under Protest, to represent the case to H. B. M. Government, hoping therefore to be justified in their proceedings, the King and Lord P.— are to have an interview next week.

Wednesday, February 22d

This evening a splendid Ball, and supper was given by the american residents here to Capt Long, and Officers of the U.S. Ship "Boston" in commeration of the birth of Gen George Washington. the hall was decorated in Flags of nearly all nations. at each end of the dancing room, hung the portraits of Washington, encircled with "Stars & Stripes", hanging down in graceful folds, nearly touching the floor. It was kept up till 5 O.c. in the morning by the gentlemen, singing songs, dancing, drinking toasts &c. we then formed a section of two front of the hall and escorted the Officers down to Reynolds Wharf where the boats were ready to receive them, and when at a short distance from the wharf, they rested on their oars while we gave them "Hail Collumbia" which was returned by three good hearty cheers. we paraded the streets with a band of music till near daylight, when each one retired to their respective homes.

Saturday, February 25th.

Lord P. has lately had several interviews with the King and after urging some of the most oppressive, and unjust demands, on him, till he was unable to comply with them, he took the only steps that could be expected from a Mighty, and Piratical Empire, when it has the advantage over a weak government. one of his demands was $80.000. and as it was not complied with, he landed his marines from the frigate at 3 O.c P.M. and marched into the fort and took possession. the soldiers surrounded the flag-staff while the proclamation was read, and then the S. I. flag [13] was pulled down by the 2d Lieut of the frigate, with the utmost spite, and vengence and the "Blood Red" flag of England was immediately hoisted, where once planted, waves forever. The observatories, verandas, and ramparts of the fort, and streets, were crowded with people, to witness the outrageous act of Great Britain, *robing* the King of his peaceful, and quiet government   the King was so affected at the time that he lost all power of speech 'tis well he might, where is there one that would not be more, or less affected, under such circumstances. God send that I may live to see the downfall of that tyrannical Empire.

Monday February 27th.

I attended a splendid party to night on bourd of the "Boston" given to the american residents here by Capt Long and the Ward Room Officers.   the supper table groaned under the weight of everything that was good, rich, and nice.   it was "kept up" by the gentlemen, (after the ladies left) till after four O.c. in the morning, and a glorious time we had I tell you, the utmost cordiality, kindness, and attention was shown us by the entertainers and I can say that I enjoyed myself better than I ever did at any other party of the kind. *War,* and *splendid parties,* seems to be order of the day here at present.

---

[13] When Captain George Vancouver visited the Hawaiian Islands in 1794, he ingratiated himself with King Kamehameha by his good counsel, even to the extent of patching up a quarrel between the chieftain and his favorite wife, with the result that the King willingly placed the Islands under the protection of Great Britain and hoisted the flag that Vancouver so generously presented to him. The British government made the great mistake of not confirming the Captain's action and in 1812 King Kamehameha created a flag of his own, using the British Union Jack for the canton and eight white, red and blue stripes to represent the eight principal islands. (Foster Rhea Dulles, *America in the Pacific,* N.Y., 1932, p. 147.)

Friday March 10th.
I attended a splended party to night at Capt Carters, given by him, to the Capt, & Officers of the "Boston" the party "came off" with the utmost hilarity, the gentlemen kept it up till near daylight with their usual good merriment, and gayety.

Tuesday March 14th,
I went to another Grand Ball again to night given by Capt Brewer, it was kept up late, but carying it to such excess had entirely beat me out, so I returned to my room to sleep, at 2 O.c. in the morning, soon after I arose from the supper table.

Wednesday March 15th.
To day the "Don Quixote" arrived 29 days from California. Aunt Mary Ann & John Henry are in good health and spirits. it seems pleasant to see them here again after a long passage of eight months.

Friday 17th.
This morning early the Behering from the U. States rounded too off Diamond Head and took a pilot. the wind being favourable she came to an anchor in about half an hour outside the harbour, the pilot then immediately came on shore and brought the letters, and I had the pleasure of receiving three long letters from my dear Sister, one from Cousin Caroline, one from Sylvia, and one from G. White, excuse me awhile for I am impatient to read them, they are all lying open on the desk before me and look rather inviting.

Every-body is congratulating me on having such a handful of letters from home, on enquiring I find that no one has got letters from Plymouth but myself which seems somewhat singular. your letters were all very interesting indeed, and I was pleased to hear of the arrival of my letters safe to hand. About your miniature, I shall expect it by the Delaware in about two months, for I entertain an eager desire to see that sweet little countenance again, do not have it flattered (as you say) by no means but send it in all its original beauty.

By news received a few days ago from Tahiti, we are acquainted with the enmity existing between the French, & English there, as regards taking possession of those islands.   the state of affairs appears to be more critical there than at this place, but we are expecting French vessels of war here every day from Tahiti to hoist the French flag on these islands, to resent the injuries pretended to have been suffered by them at the Society Islands.   if such should be the case it would terminate, only, in violence, and blood-shed, as the case now stands.   these two groups of islands must be declared independent by the two countries England, and France, or a war must evidently be the result, time will decide.

By your letters I find that all the pretty Plymouth girls are getting married off fast. I must bear a hand and get home, to win one of the fairy nymphs over to my affections. It is difficult telling when I shall be among you again, it depends altogether on circumstances, and the result of this national affair.   if the English should continue to hold possession of these islands, we shall bid farewell to this place in about two years. I dread the idea of leaving these islands, for the climate agrees with me, and I enjoy myself here much.

Cousin Martha Ann presented her husband [with] a fine little girl on the   th inst – it has [not] been named yet. Nelly Blue is still the same blooming little rose as ever,

I must now bring my letter to a conclusion for I have got to the end of my sheet, and the Wm Gray sails tomorrow morning.

Letters from Honolulu, 1841-1845

Give my love to father, John & Herbert, Grand'thr and all my friends, and acquaintences, at home, and now with every sentiment of affection, and grattitude, I remain ever dear Sister

Your Affectionate Brother
James

[pr "Miceno"   Capt Clark
Will Mess. E. T. Loring & Co. please forward this]

Honolulu, Sand'ch Islands, June 16, 43
To Miss Frances A. Gleason, Plymouth.
My Dear Sister,

I improve this opportunity offered by the Barque "Miceno" bound to Valparaiso to write you a few lines which to hand, will inform you of my good health, hoping you are enjoying the same good blessing. – The "Blood Red" flag of England (which bears the stains of her character) still continues to wave, and the English to rule over us. Not only has this Lord Paulet succeeded in taking possession of these Islands in a most cruel manner, but is, and always has been ever since the first day he arrived here, trying all in his power to injure the Americans and the American interest in the place. I would like to see him meet with that punishment he so justly deserves, but we can hardly hope for it, as this is only a criterion of all the rest of the barbarious acts that so disgrace the annals of England.

I bought me a fine little steed a few days ago and as Uncle William has moved up to his country seat in the Valley for the summer I ride in every night at sunset after the store is closed to tea, and spend the evening it is a lovely spot, and one knows well how to appreciate the comfort of such a rural and luxuriant place in a bright moonlight evening after suffering from the effects of a burning sun, dust, and musqueters during the day.

We shall begin to look for the arrival of the Brig "Delaware" in a few days, by her I shall expect lots of letters from home. I have not received any since the Bhering arrived, three months, so a letter from you now would be very acceptable. I shall expect by her too your miniature

Aunt Mary Ann presented us with a fine little Cousin, a girl, on the   of last month. I expect we shall have girls enough introduced here soon to organize a dancing school among ourselves, preparations are going on here among the Yankees for celebrating the 4th of July in grand style, a splendid dinner is to be given and it is not decided upon yet whether a Ball and super will be given in the evening or not. I think we shall carry it out to the full extent. I am in hopes to enjoy myself equally as well as if I were at home among you.

The very great improbability of this not reaching you for six or eight months to come will account, and I hope excuse me for not writing lengthy and to my friends in Plymouth, please remember me to them all and tell them to write long letters by every opportunity to their friends at the S. Islands.

I doubt whether Aunt Mary, and Martha Ann will write by this opportunity for they have got *"such* a family to take care of" (as Uncle William says) and being completely discouraged by not receiving letters from home by the two or three last vessels [which] have arrived. I received six by the last.   how I ca[n] crow. We have receipts from the U. States up to the 28th of Feb'y, we learn that the U.S. Government have acknowledged these Islands an independent Gov't

Letters from Honolulu, 1841-1845

through the exertions of Haalilio (the King's[14] Embassador) and Mr. Richards,[15] who left here sometime since for the purpose of obtaining the Independence of these Islands   they are to visit America, England, & France. God grant that they may be equally as successfull in England, & France, as they have been in Congress.[16]

---

[14] The reign of King Kamehameha III was the longest in the history of Hawaii and was filled with wise accomplishments. His wisdom and fine traits of character were rewarded by the love and devotion of his subjects. (*Biographical Sketches of Hawaii's Rulers,* by the Bishop National Bank of Hawaii, p. 9.)

[15] The Reverend William Richards was a Christian minister, an educator, diplomat, and a dynamic force in the upbuilding of the Islands. He was the first Minister of Education in the cabinet of King Kamehameha III. (*Lahaina Historical Guide,* by The Maui Historical Society, p. 34.)

[16] It is strange to realize that at this time Hawaii, more than California, was the ripened apple to the eyes of foreign powers. An American resident of Honolulu wrote in 1843, "If the fair bud which has thus far been fostered by American citizens is not matured and strengthened by the government, a rival nation will pluck the fruit."

The security of the Islands had been threatened in 1839 when France, incensed at a law banning Catholic priests from the Islands, dispatched the 48-gun *Artemise* with Captain La Place, who threatened to bombard the town unless the Hawaiians accepted an ultimatum recognizing Catholicism. He prophesied that "the Sandwich Islands will some day belong to the masters of California."

While the Hawaiian Commissioners Haalilio (the King's ambassador) and Mr. Richards were on a mission to America, England and France, to secure guarantees of the independence of the Hawaiian Islands, England sent Alexander Simpson to Hawaii to act as consul. The King refused to receive him, which brought down the ire of Captain Lord Paulet of the *H.M.S. Carysfort.* The Hawaiian flag was hauled down and the British flag took its place while Paulet even formed a native regiment, "The Queen's Own," officered by British subjects but paid for out of the Hawaiian treasury.

The Hawaiian king appealed for aid from the United States and the State Department lost no time in giving it. A strong protest was made to England with the result that John Bull disavowed Paulet's action and upon the visit of Rear-Admiral Thomas USN in 1843, there was a formal lowering of the British flag and hoisting of the Hawaiian ensign. The complete independence of the Islands was reaffirmed. It was only natural that the Hawaiian government should place its faith in the United States rather than in France or England, and there was a feeling in the Islands that American annexation was the only way to free the Islands of the threat of foreign aggression. The

Again I remind you of remembering me to all my friends at home. Aunt Mary & Martha Ann and Uncle William send their love.

   Your affectionate Brother   James. H.

[Barth'w (Bartholomew) Gosnold, Capt Russell letter address:
Capt. James G. Gleason, Plymouth, Mass.]

         Honolulu July 28th 1843
To Miss Frances A. Gleason, Plymouth
My Dear Sister

I have just seen Capt Russell the bearer of this letter, says that he has declined sailing untill after Monday [31st] which will be a glorious day here and a day that will ever be remembered by every American resident here with fond recollections. Admiral Thomas had an interview with the King to day he told him that his flag should be hoisted on Monday at 10 O.c. A.M. and likewise be saluted by every vessel of War in port, being the U.S. Ship Constellation, H. B. M. Ship Dublin, H. B. M. S. Carysfort, & H. B. M. Ship Hazard, the merchant vessels and whaleships in port will also hoist the S. I. Flag and join in the salute, all the Stores in the village will be closed that every one may join in celebrating the day, hasty preparations are going on among the American residents to raise a splended dinner by subscription it is to be at the French Consul's hall close by the fort where the flag is to be hoisted, what a glorious time we will have, hip! hip! hurah!

United States' Secretary of State wrote, "The Hawaiian Pear's now fully ripe, and this is the golden hour for the United States to pluck it," but the ripened pear was not plucked until August 12, 1898, when both houses of Congress passed the annexation resolution and it was approved by President McKinley. (Dulles, *America in the Pacific,* pp. 148-49.)

how cheap Lord Paulet must feel, to be compelled to salute the flag that he has trampled on so much Hip! hip! hurah! again for that. what a complete overthrow.

I attended a splended party night before last, given by Mrs Dominis at her house. the Officers of the U.S.S. Constellation, & H. B. M. S. Hazard, were invited and accepted the invitation, the King and Governors of Oahu, and Maui, were also present, we danced till about 2 O.c. and spent the few remaining hours of the night singing songs. the ladies here are all married, not one *Single One* is there mariageble among them, consequently they get beat out about midnight and retire as has always proved at the parties heretofore, but night before last they seemed to enjoy themselves so well that they remained till near daylight and departed with the gentlemen. I forget to say that a splended supper was provided for the occasion.

The two little nameless responsibilities at the house are flourishing rapidly, they grow prettier every day. John Henry and Nelly Blue have got to be very interesting little children they can talk, fight, and quarel equal to any of their age. I have looked around for something that I might present to you and my friends at home, in a manner more tangible than words, but there is nothing but what is common at home, and double the price, I am in hopes when Capt Dominis arrives from China (who is expected in a few months) to be able to obtain something which might be worthy of your acceptance.

I was much disappointed in not getting your miniature by the "Delaware." I fear that there will not be another opportunity to send it for sometime, but I shall centre my hopes in the next vessel that arrives here from home. I shall not only expect yours but Cousin Caroline's. I thank her very kindly for her long and interesting letter to me   I shall answer it by this opportunity if I can possibly get time, give my best love to her, her brother, Aunt & Uncle Cooper, Grandmother, Sylvia, and all my friends at home.   not forgetting Mrs Sylvesters and her family.

Give my respects to George White, tell him I thank him for his kind letter but shall not be able to answer it by this vessel.   tell him to keep up a stiff upper lip till I get home, and not let the Plymouth lasses get to the windward of him if he does he is lost beyond recovery.

Your Affectionate Brother
James

P. S. Tomorrow night there is to be a splended ball at the Mansion House, on Friday this King gives a public dinner, and sometime during next week there will be a ball on board the U.S. Ship Constellation and likewise on board the Dublin   hip! hip! hurah!!
J. H. G.

RESTORATION ANTHEM
Hail to our rightful King
We joyful honor bring
  This day to thee,
Long live your Majesty,
Long reign this Dynasty,
And for Posterity,
  Thy sceptre be,
Hail to the worthy name,
Worthy his country's fame,
  Thomas the brave.
Long shall thy virtues be
Shrined in our memory,
Who come to set us free,
  Quick o'er the wave.

Praise to our heavenly King,
To thee our thanks we bring,
Worthy of all.
Loud we thine honors raise,
Loud is our song of praise,
Smile on our future days,
Sovereign of all.
(Tune – "God Save the Queen")

The above piece of poetry was composed by a resident here and sung by the young Chiefs on the day of the restoration of the Sandwich Islands and also at the Public dinner given to the King in Nuuanu Valley.

Honolulu   Sand'ch Islds   Sept 8/43

To Miss Frances A. Gleason, Plymouth

My Dear Sister,

The Barque "Bhering" Capt Snow bound for the U. States offered me another opportunity to write to my dear sister which I embrace with much pleasure I am enjoying exceedingly good health and the exercise that I have in riding out to the country seat in Nuuanu Valley in the evening to tea fully compensates for the close confinement and dull monotony of the store during the day. I can hardly keep my eyes open to day being on board the U.S.S. Cyane last night till nearly four O.c. this morning at a splended Ball, and a grand and glorious time we had. I had formed an acquaintance with nearly all of the Officers previous to receiving my invitation, and as I prepared on board in the evening about nine O.c. I was received in the gangway by several of the superior Officers most cordially I assure you, and as I passed aft on to the quarter deck trimmed so splendedly for the Ball-room, I met with several midshipmen that I had become intimately acquainted with on shore ready to welcome me with joy and eager to take me by the arm and show me round in different parts of the ship the cabin, ward-room, steerage, and on the poop where the rich, and neat supper tables were spread &c. I was highly delighted with the manner in which the dances were conducted, and likewise the way in which the deck was trimmed for the occasion, flags of nearly all nations encircled the Ballroom, and the noble brass capstan surrounded with muskets with candles deposited in the muzzles while the steel bayonets polished so brightly answered for reflecters. I danced nearly every dance and enjoyed myself well, but there is one thing very much wanting which to have it would make our frequent parties shine, that is the want of *young* ladies, there is but one in the place and ugly looking as she is, she is considered the belle of the village, there is just enough married ladies the wives of merchants here that dance to fill two sets of cotillions which makes a party pass off aggreeably, but not so much so were there an addition of young girls to entertain the young men who feel (as it is natural) a sort of diffidence while in the society of people far their superiors. the party broke up about half past three O.c. in the morning and after passing the "Good-night!" I left the ship they earnestly requesting me to call off and visit them as often as I could make it convenient. On the 25th of last July I attended a large and splended party given by Mrs. Dominis, and on the 4th of Aug I was present at another at the Mansion House given by the Officers of the U.S.S. Constellation the Officers of the H. B. M. Ships Dublin & Hazard and the U.S. Ships Cyane and United States [17] were

---

[17] At the end of the Revolutionary War, the United States had sold all of her warships that had not been sunk or captured and this now powerful nation owned not a single armed vessel. At the urgings of President Washington, six frigates were built in 1797-1798, three of which, the *Constitution, Constella-*

present which made quite a large party, another party was given by Mrs Hooper (the Am Consul's lady) on the 25 of last month, so you see that we are going to extremes on parties and in fact it has been a glorious time in Honolulu ever since the Restoration of the Old Flag soon after the King had his Islands restored to him he gave a Public dinner at his Country Seat in Nuuanu Valley about five miles from town the dinner was "got up" on strict temperance principles, lemonade was the strongest drink, the tables were spread in the grove and a lovely spot it is too the tall and slender trees so straight, and orderly, waving too, and fro, in the light breeze like weeping willows, affording us a good cool shade from a burning sun, it was a gay sight too to see us all riding into town together towards night on horse back upwards of two thousand people, men, women, and children,

I send you as a present by this vessell a gold Pencil Case. the fact of everything being so high here prevents me from making those presents that I would make were they to be purchased reasonable. the Pencil Case that I send is valued here at $8. whereas it could be bought at home probably for four and so it is with every imported article one hundred % must be realized on the original cost to defray the expenses of a long voyage.

Uncle William has had considerable business for the last five or six months. he is (which you have probably heard before this) Collector of Customs for this port, and licensed Auctioneer which keeps him pretty

---

tion and *United States,* visited the Pacific. The *Constellation* carried 36 guns and distinguished herself during the French War by capturing the frigate *Insurgente* and defeating the frigate *Vengeance* which, however, escaped into the night. (Frank C. Bowen, *The Sea: Its History & Romance,* 4 vols., N.Y., 1927, III, p. 151.)

closely employed, he also a few days ago very unexpectedly had the consignment of a vessel's cargo from Sidney he has already sold (in eight days) about $8000. the commissions of the entire cargo will put into his pocket the fine little sum of 500. to 600.$ which to him is quite a God-send. I know of nothing more to add to this but if I should before the Bhering sails I will put it on another sheet.

Give my love to Father & Brothers Grand'r Sylvia Aunt and Uncle Cooper Cousin Caroline and Edward I shall expect a letter from each of them by the return of the Bhering and likewise from *fifteen* to *twenty five* pages from yourself.

Your Affectionate Brother James
[first page margin note] Please divide the china engravings between Edward, John & Herbert.

[Per "Bhering" Capt Snow]
Honolulu Oahu Sand'ch Islds
Sept 10th 1843

My Dear Sister,

As the Bhering will remain here some time yet waiting for a cargo I shall continue to keep a brief daily Journal and note down passing events such as rise uppermost in my mind and you must keep this point constantly in view viz that I am not writing for the world merely to my dear Sister

Sunday Sept 10th

Rode out in the Valley in the morning and spent the day reading "Souvenirs of a residence in Europe" in the afternoon about 5 O.c. I rode into town and went off on board the U.S.S. Cyane to pay a visit as I had been pressed very hard of late by my friends on board to call off and see them   I spent an hour there pleasantly in conversation and then went on board the Bhering and took tea with Mr Knox (1 mate) in the evening I went to church and heard Mr S. Damon preach after meeting was over I called on Mrs. Sullivan and spent the evening with her till near half past nine O.c. Mr Whiting of the Cyane was present.

Monday, 11th

To day the U.S. Store Ship Erie arrived 31 days from Callio with Commodore Dallas on board who has come out here from the U. States to relieve Com'r Jones in command of the Pacific Squadron who is ordered home to be tried by a Court Martial in consequence of taking and giving up possession of Monterey in October last   it will evidently go very hard against Com'r Jones when he arrives home by his conduct out here he has heard that Com'r Dallas is out here to relieve him and contrary to the principles of a man of deep sound sence and judgement is trying all in his power to avoid him and likewise those places where he is suspicious despatches are awaiting him from Com'r Dallas it is with feelings of regret mingled with pity that we consider his circumstances   he has heretofore shown himself zealous and patriotic in his country cause and that he should now rise up and commit an act so degrading to our navy and so deeply injurious to the American interest throughout California is to us a matter of no little wonder and surprise   he will in all probability be discharged from the navy and I do not think that I judge harshly of him when I say that thus had ought to be his punishment without *cerimony*.

The "Erie" immediately on coming to anchor outside the reef was saluted by the U.S.S. Cyane with guns. In the evening I took tea with Mr Wilson at the

Mansion House   I was there introduced by him to Mr Robinson & Mr Poor Officers of the Erie.

Tuesday 12th

To day at 11 Oc the Comodore flag was removed from the Erie to the Cyane and a salute fired on the occasion. At 12 Oc Admiral Thomas called on board to pay his respects to the Commodore and was saluted with the usual number of guns. I have been interested during the day reading "A tale of our Ancestors"   "by a Lady of Virginia"   I have been reading so many light works Affecting tales love Stories &c lately that in taking up a History I cannot feel the least interest in it whatever   I took up Cooper's Naval History a new publication the other day with a determination to read it through hearing that it was an entertaining work but had hardly got through the first volume when I threw it down in despair but then it is a work that a person can resume at intervals and feel as deep an interest in it as ever   I spent the most of the evening at home with quite a large company   I bid them all "good night" about 9 O.c. and was on the point of mounting my horse to ride into town when I was alarmed by a terrible screaching of the ladies behind me and on looking round I saw them all running out of the house thinking something serious had happened I went in and judge my surprise on finding that about a hundred cock-roaches had introduced themselves into the room at that moment and flying about in all directions which to say (speaking within bounds) the smallest of them were an inch and a half long and were dealing a furious battle with the gentlemen   some of them would take a curious fancy (I dont know what made them) to pounce down upon the lilly white necks of the ladies which would consequently cause them to spring up in the air about *ten* feet and cry for mercy   the battle lasted about fifteen minutes and finding that none of the challenged party were killed or injured they prepaired again to their favorite amusement whist that they were so unpleasantly disturbed from and I to my journey

Wednesday 13th

Nothing worthy of note during the day   I had the store closed at sunset as usual and mounted my horse and rode out in the valley to tea   it being a dark and unpleasant evening and no visiters in the valley I mounted my horse and rode into town again immediately after tea   I first prepaired to the Mansion House on arriving in town, Capt Penhallow was the only occupant   he was sitting in a private room leaning over his desk with his head rest on his hand apparently in very deep thought so much so that my entrance and salutation were quite unnoticed   I advanced towards him and again bid him "good evening" "you are in very deep thought" I remarked   "yes" he replied "I was thinking of that poor fellows friends at home that I am intimately acquainted with that was wounded in a duel this afternoon"   I was taken all aback as you may suppose for it was the first time I had heard anything about it and the first time a duel was ever fought on the Islands   he handed me a pair of pistoles out of the desk he was sitting by and said that they were the very weapons the duel was fought with and that he handed them to the Seconds after they left the house after dinner thinking they had nought but innocent intentions.   the duelists were John P. Decatur and Stanwood Gansevort midshipmen of the "Erie"   it seems that some animosity existed between them and they went out in the valley to settle it in this deadly manner.   nine shots were exchanged between the parties without taking effect but the tenth wounded the former in the leg just below the knee   it is thought that the leg will have to be amputated   this standing up for a shooting mark to my view is rather a serious matter   I would be excused anytime.

After I left the Mansion House I went down to I. Anthous room and played whist till nearly 10 O.c. and by an extraordinary run of good luck we beat our opponents far better players than our selves two games while they beat us one.

Thursday 14th
Engaged in various duties about the store during the day   I spent the forepart of the evening at Mrs Dominis playing "Soltare"   after I left I went down to Mr Roneys room and spent the remainder of the evening with him in conversation   with him till near 10 O.c   Mr. Roney is a midshipman on board the U.S.S. Cyane   he is a fine young man and a pleasant and aggreeable associate   he is living on shore at present in consequence of ill-health   he informed me that Mr Decatur was much worse to day and that the doctor had been attempting to extract the ball but did not succeed.   the duelists were put under arrest last night and the prevailing opinion was that they would be sent home and suspended from the navy but fortunately Commodore Dallas put them on duty again so they are O.K. once more.

Saturday 16th
To day I was invited to go on board the Cyane by my friend Mr Wilson to dine with him   I prepaired on board at 12 Oc and remained till nearly 3 Oc in the afternoon. I rode out in the valley to tea at sunset and spent the evening.

Saturday Nov'r 10th 1843

Being so busy for the last month I have not had time to continue my journal and as the Bhering sails on the first of next week I must bring my letter to a close, if I have time I shall write to Father. Aunt Mary Ann says that I must write something about her *baby* I hardly know what to say, merely that she is an angel she resembles you so much that she thinks of naming it Frances which she will with the husband's consent. John Henry and Nelly Blue quarell, and fight as much as ever, they are just getting old enough to know what *justice* is, Nelly being so stought most generally comes off conquerer. John Henry will at times be running into the house with tears in his eyes crying out "Mama! mama! Nelly's been knocking me down" and the only satisfaction he gets under these circumstances is to be shut up in a dark room. Love to all again.

Your Affectionate Brother, James H.

[pr "Wm & Eliza" Capt Rogers]

Honolulu Sand'ch Islands
December 10th 1843

To Miss Frances A Gleason, Plymouth
My Dear Sister

The Wm & Eliza bound for the U. States offers me another direct opportunity which I gladly avail myself of and am in fact duty bound also to write to my dear Sister as report said that the Wm & Eliza was to sail tomorrow morning, I intended to have devoted this long winter evening in writing an epistle to you equally as long. But I have this moment (noon) heard that she sails about 5 O.c. this afternoon unavoidably I must sit down now amidst the hurry and excitement of business and scratch off a few hurried lines. It is but a few days since that I closed sundry letters sent by the Bhering written to sundry friends at home combining sundry pages somewhere in the neighbourhood of six & twenty consequently I have exhausted myself or in the technical phrase written myself out.

The chest of presents and curiosities that was intended to have been sent by the Bhering was with-held to be forwarded by this opportunity in consequence of some unnecessary trouble that would have attended it. I sent you a gold pencil case and Cousin Caroline an embroidered apron and some Chino pictures for Edward John & Herbert and likewise nine grass cloth Handkfs three for Caroline three for Sylvia and three for yourself.   the Handkerchiefs are not very fine but still they are the best that can be obtained here at present.

It is now mid-winter and you at home now are undoubtedly wrapped up in your thick clocks and mittens puffing and blowing while we are here dressed in our simple suit of linen and the sun pouring down its radient beams upon us almost hot enough to burn us up everything looks fresh and green flowers in bloom fruit ripening &c what a contrast – I have got so naturalized to warm weather that I fear if I should undertake to spend a winter among you I should freeze to death.

Mr Cummins an intimate friend of mine is going passenger in this vessel   he thinks of visiting Plymouth if you should meet with him he will give you considerable information concerning the youth in the employ of Paty & Co. with

"———————————— those ringlets
Curled half down his neck so bare" – Get out

The Ship has hawled stem-too and her topsails loosed consequently I must close for want of time   Give my love to all enquiring friends Father, Brothers, Grand-

mother Sylvia Aunt & Uncle Cooper Cousin Caroline
& Edward G. White &c. &c.
>	Ever Your Affectionate Brother
>	James

[favd by Capt Sherman
W. Ship "Nimrod" U.S.A.]   [July 29th 1844]

>	To my Sister

>	1

My Sister! my Sweet Sister, far from thee,
Reluctant have I strayed. — This distant isle
Has been my dwelling place, and still will be
Till years have passed away, — when thy glad smile
Will fondly greet me to my humble home,
An exile doomed from thence to wander, and to roam,

>	2

But now it has become my lot to dwell
In climes more genial than our northern Shores,
Could I but have thee here my heart would swell,
In gladness and forget awhile my native bowers.
But ah! to be, — to live, — to roam again,
Upon my native soil! it is my lasting — deep — unfaultering aim

>	3

I now would ask thee Sister is it true
That peace and calm contentment 'round thee dwell
Alas I fear me not for once I knew
And still do fear there is an earthly H-ll
You know of whom I speak so let it pass
God send she may have changed or will so do while yet
  her life may last.

>	4

My playmates where are they I fancying see
Them all assembled on our Plymouth Green
The hoop, — the bat and ball, — O! could I be
Again linked with thier sports and sweet fifteen
But Ah! those days are passed the stream impetuously
Rolls on and bears me hence to manhoods troubled sea.

5

There's Geor-ge White with cheeks of rosy red
I wander if sweet Cxxxxxxx has ever pressed
Her lips to those   my stars what have I said
I beg ten thousand pardons George but blessed
Is he who with so sweet a one doth stray
Out to Cold Spring, or Hobbs-Hole brook, or
    where thier path may lay

6

And then those evening parties Sweet to me
Were hours spent thus untill a midnight hour
We "turned the cover" played the "Juniper tree"
And if some girls were kissed how awful sour
They'd look as if to peirce you through
While others temper'd sweet — blushingly would yeald —
    receive thier due,

7

Seventeen long months have passed no word from home
In that wide lapse of time has come to hand
If good or ill betide thee — as the stone
So all to me is hushed till ocean waves may land
Upon this island shore a welcome line
From thee in thine own hand alas! with hope
    I wile away the time

    But hark! Sail O! is echoed far and wide
    The "Congress" [18] long looked for has arrived
    She rounds bold Diamond Point the anchorage nigh
    To brace the yards the sailors quickly fly
    With circling way she luffs up to the breeze
    Receives on deck the Pilot of these Seas
    Her course again resum'd She swiftly glides
    Into the bay 'midst strong and varying tides
    Unmindful though of these with press of sail
    She stems the tide and reels before the gale
    "Stand by the anchor"! shouts the Pilot now
    The second in command flies to the bow

---

[18] The frigate *Congress* was launched at Portsmouth Navy Yard in 1841 and ended her career in 1862 at Hampton Roads when she was sunk by the Confederate steam ram *Merrimac*. Her utter helplessness from the attack of the ironclad marked the passing of the sailing man-of-war. (Bowen, *The Sea: Its History & Romance,* III, p. 152; IV, p. 110.)

And with a careful hand doth quick unlose
And firm he holds it with a single noose
Sail after sail reduc'd with slackened pace
She mooves on proudly to the anchoring place
The anchoring place now gained — her anchor down
Quick round she swings her stern towards the town,
All safe secur'd the Pilot then descends
Into his boat — lik reeds the oars bend
The boat comes dashing onward near and near
And people gather thick upon the pier
The boat has gained the shore and with a bound
The Pilot springs and lands upon the ground
The bulky bag whose contents sweetly dear
Is passed from Hand to Hand upon the pier
Backed by a stout Kanaka on it goes
Into the Consuls hands, — my stars who knows
But I may have a hundred lines from home
The thought I shall not, hardly can be bourne
But soon we'll see what luck I have in store
The bag o'erturn'd its contents forth do pour
Twice, — thrice I've over-hawled the glossy pile
Not one sole line from home I'll wait a while
Perchance there may be in the vessels hold
A box containing treasures yet untold
But ah! how vain the thought, a week has pass'd
The hope I cherish'd has grown cold at last,

But let us chang the scene come mount with me
Our steeds and ride far inland from the sea
Nuuanu Valley — there we'll wend our way
Till the calm eve setts in we there will stay
The mountains on each hand are towering high
Five miles before us does the Pali lie
With gentle pace we urge our steeds along
A mile is passed   shall we go further on
No let us stop — dismount for we've arriv'd
At a neat cottage by the mountains side
Ah no! I'm wrong a steep descent and brook
Divides it widely from the mountain foot
How tastefully laid out the path is wide
An angle turn'd we then see on each side
A garden square and cut into the ground

Is paths one forms a cross the other round
And in each quarter of the wheel does peek
Out from the bushy leaves the strawberry sweet
Outside "the wheel (we call it) with a cross
Trees in the light breeze thier branches toss
Perfumes of flowers — geraniums we exhale
As all around they're playing in the gale
The velvet turf springs thickly at our feet
And everything around looks trim and neat
The weather fine, — the doors wide open swing
And loudly hear we laugh that merry one
Of Nelly Blue I speak — we'll go awhile
And with that playful one few hours beguile
But where's the babe that sweet angelic one
Born to the world scarce seen two summers sun
Our cousin Caroline Frances   She is dead
Her angel soul to other realms has fled
Where has she gone we ask of little Ellen
Mournfully she'll answer "Gone to Heaven"
She was her parents pride thier tenderest love
May we when called to die meet her above,

Concluding Stanzas

1

When the sun sinks to rest and the broad moon has brightened
    And all Nature is breathing in silent repose
Then by the murmuring brook I delight to awaken
    Those thoughts that in rapture my soul only knows.

2

Those thoughts, dearly kind, often-times do they wander,
    O'er mountains and seas that divide me from thee,
And peirce the sweet home that I cherish so tender,
    Where'er in this torturing world I may be.

3

Sweet sister, adieu! for on the eve of departing,
    Is the ship that bears onward these stanzas to thee
May breezes blow fair, — blow fresh, — and blow lasting,
    And shorten her distance upon the blue sea,

4
Give my love to all friends, and to all my relations,
　　　Ever with them I would fain hope to be,
To gain gold! sordid gold! drives me from my own nation
　　　With a tear do I name it, for that I've left thee,
　　　　　　　　　　　　Your Affectionate Brother
　　　　　　　　　　　　　　　　　　James

To Miss Frances A. Gleason, Plymouth Mass.
July 29th 1844

I have unfolded this letter to acknowledge the receipt of your letter by the Globe likewise one from Herbert and father. Please excuse me to father for not writing to him by this opportunity for the excitement of the last three days has completely upset me, it is the first anniversary of the Restoration of these islands by Admiral Thomas – The music – garlands, Flowers, snow white robes, sparkling eyes, white arms, braids, and bracelets, swan like bosoms, &c. &c. are floating in rapid succession through my imagination consequently it is a matter of impossibility for me to calm myself down to pen one sober word.
　　　　　　　Yours Affectionately　　　James
Aug 3d /44

[pr "Inez", Capt Knox
　Care of Capt. Ja's G. Gleason]
　　　　　　　　　　Honolulu　Hawaiian Islands
　　　　　　　　　　　　　　　March 18, 1845
To Miss Frances A. Gleason
My Dear Sister

Head winds have detained the "Inez" which offers me an opportunity to inscribe a few lines. What shall I say? Here I sit to my silver bound rose wood writing desk　　on one hand hanging up against the wall in a large gilt frame is "Love in a Cottage" on the other is "Caroline" bending over the balcony gazing on the Queen of Night. Lovely representations of the poetry of life. I attended temperance meeting a few evenings since and heard an excellent address delivered by the Rev Geo. Jones chaplain of the U.S. Frigate "Brandywine"[19] now lying at this port.   on arriving at the hall the band from the frigate was playing a very spirited air and a crowded audience had assembled which told that the power which influenced such happy results in civilized lands was beginning to be felt in these remote isles of the Pacific. The walls sparkled with painted fountains and flowing liquid from capsised brandy casks, which added strength to the cause, and *beauty to the walls.* 'Tis sweet to listen to the flow of eloquence, Sweet to hear the drunkard's life painted to us in its most thrilling, and startling form by a powerful mind and watch its intended effect upon the inebriate. 'Tis sweet to gaze on falling cascades, sparkling fountains, and broken brandy casks, – Sweet to see a drunkard sign the pledge – Music is sweet   But sweeter far than *this* than *all,* is to gaze upon a pretty girl! Bernice was seated at a short distance from me to the left and as no object intervened, I had a commanding view of those jet black ringlets just commingling – just dividing, falling down a neck of the most perfect symetry, in the language of the poet

> "You'd swear each clustering lock could feel
> "And curl to give her neck caresses."

---

[19] The frigate *Brandywine* was attached to the sloop-of-war *Vincennes* on her first good will tour around the world in 1826, visiting Hawaii and other Pacific ports, and became the first United States warship to circumnavigate the globe. The *Vincennes* made two more such tours and was one of our most traveled warships. The *Brandywine* was known for her fine sailing qualities.

It seems amusing that the chaplain from a ship named the *Brandywine* should be lecturing on temperance!

She is a young chiefess! All I could do of course was to look and admire   But however I had a pleasant walk home with her after the servises were ended and deposited her safe at her Royal abode with a friendly "good night"

I have become greatly attached to these islands and if ever I leave them it will be only to return to them again perhaps a *married* man   pretty girls are in great demand here, the market is so scarce of them that people are compelled to go to other places to find a wife   It has been so long since I have heard from home that I am in doubts whether or no I am addressing a Mrs ——————— nineteen years old! the thing is possible.   how time slips away, It seems but yesterday that Plymouth shores faded from my view. nearly four years have passed since then when with a heart dancing with delight I bent myself o'er the taffrail and gazed on the fast receeding shores as our ship yealded to the influence of the gale and danced and bounded across the watery bay. I felt that I was free   I looked forward with a humble though courageous hope behind only with despair. Every bound that our ship made from billow to billow divided me more widely from that spot and it operated on my feelings like balsam to a wound, four years! and yet no change in my feelings towards that place. The same continual loathing and hatred which time serves only to strengthen. I shall revisit it once more to follow the example of my predecessor viz to snatch from it one of its pure and brightest ornaments to deck my person with through life! (what miserable paper this is)

I wish you to do me a favour, I wrote you a letter to you a short time since in verse if it should ever reach you I beg that you will destroy it at once, I hardly know what I wrote, but this much I know that selfish Providence never bestowed her poetic gifts on me. Consequently whatever I did write, must have been cold-blooded murder to the english language by throwing it into rhyme What could induce me to make such a fool of myself I know not; but however it was my first, and it shall be my last. Byron was the only that ever wrote poetry. His name will remain bright when all others fade. Remember me to all my friends.

Your Affectionate Brother.　　James

[pr "Inez", Capt Knox]

Honolulu　Sandwich Islands
March 28, 1845

To Miss Frances A. Gleason
My Dear Sister

Since closing my letter of the 17th inst the "Montreal" has ar'v'd without bringing me *one single letter* from my friends in Plymouth. It is now nearly two years since my last dates from home during which time a number of opportunities have offered for communicating. What, I ask can this deep and mysterious silence mean? What Agency is at work to torment me with the pangs of disappointment, other letters have been rec'd from Plymouth, why should I be excluded from the blessing. Have you not *one thought?* Not *one word*. Have you not *one hour* in secret to devote in writing to an absent brother? to unfold to him your feelings, your joys, or your grievances? If you have or if you have not (which latter, good heaven forbid) pray let me know, could I command the language adequate to express my feelings I would touch a cord that should jar to some purpose. Having been so often disappointed by direct arrivals from home I have in a measure become hardened to it, and it is now almost a matter of indiferance whether I receive letters or no. In glancing over the "Old Colony Memorial" I observe my father's advertisement. This is the only information I have from home in regard to 'family matters'   I have seen Mr Cummins, but I could wring nothing from him, his visit to Plymouth faded before matters of much more importance   He remembers of my father having said "that he was so busy that he could not write." and "that the girls had a great deal to say and *thought* of writing to me"! yes, they "thought of writing to me"!! This removes the curtain   This indeed unfolds the mystery; well! well! I have claim to a *thought* without a *will*. Can this be possible? is this the return for the many letters I have written? I appeal to your concience, is it kind? or is it just? But I will drop this subject and commit myself to the future, with a hope that the next arrival may bring me a line from you if not from others, which may be – G–d knows when

Yesterday passed here with great excitement. Early in the morning before daylight the remains of Haalilio H. H. M. Commissioner to the U.S. & Europe were removed from the "Montreal" to the fort. At 3 O'clock P.M. the funeral ceremony took place; the body was followed to the Rev'd Mr Armstrong's church by a large company of soldiers, foreign residents, and natives. Also the officers, marines, & seamen from the english ship of war "Talbot" now lying at this port. The corse was brought into the church and placed before the pulpet and a very affecting funeral sermon preached by the Rev'd Mr Armstrong in both english and native languages. Services being ennded the procession was again formed as before and the corse conveyed to its final resting place – the Royal tomb, there to remain in peace. On arriving at the toomb previous to depositing the body a short prayer was made; which being over the coffin was placed by the King's direction according to the usual custom. The marines fired three vollies. The guns from the fort and "Talbot" pealed forth thier thunder. And the flags among the shipping and on [sh]ore which had been lowered half mast out [of] sympathy for the nation's loss, again resumed thier places at the mast head. This is the end of human greatness   The loss of this worthy native cannot be sufficiently lamented, he possessed a strong and comprehensive mind, and this well stored as it was with the manners & customs of enlightened nations; he would have been a brilliant star in the firmament of state affairs in the Hawaiian Kingdom had it been destined for him to return in health to his native home. The loss will be most sensibly felt by this young & flourishing nation. I learn that he visited Plymouth and my friends if so you cannot but have been highly pleased with him.

[The following letter was crossed at right angles to the previous one.] /March 30/ On the point of closing this letter Wm Carver stepped into my room very unexpectedly and notified me that he was direct from home and had several boxes on board the ship for me which was lying in the outer harbor. This was indeed glorious news, I had a boat manned immediately and went off to get them. I returned with the *treasures* and having locked myself in my room to guard against interruption commenced operations   in my eagerness to get the covers off I stove the sides and ends of the boxes in and mangled them in a most brutal manner and completely rendered them unfit for further service. Had there been an observer present I presume to say that he would have stared in the greatest bewilderment at the savage manner in which I was operating on an old wooden box I must have appeared to him like a person that had been starved out and just obtained a box of *meat*. But however ungainly I may have conducted myself never once entered my mind for I had a grand object in view. The box as you may suppose yielded to my strength and fell to pieces with the most surprising swiftness; having possessed myself of my own "personal property" I forthwith despatched the ballance off to Uncle Wm's and I seated myself [in] a most pleasant business. I do not remember of crying over a letter before in my life but I must say that on this occasion the pleasure heightened as it was by a long interval of silence and disappointments, the tears sparkling and bright would ascend from the fountain of sympathy and fall glittering on your tender lines before me in spite of all my endeavors to restrain them. Your letter was the longest and certainly the most beautiful composition that I have ever received from you and I severely reproach myself for having penned that which I would gladly wish this red ink might serve to blot out and render uninteligable. I ought to tear this letter to pieces but that I cannot do, when I once commience I am like that beautiful appelation which the english apply to Daniel Webster "a steam car in breetches" which signifies go ahead! but I implore you my own dear forgiving sister, pass it by without giving it a thought, It was wrote in one of those moods that people speak of when one feels seriously inclined to "tear his shirt" and bite off the heads of 20d Nails!!   but in an hour of cool reflection we bitterly reproach ourselves for our foolishness. Your advise is indeed very kind in regard to temperance: you advise me to sign the pledge. I am sorry to say that it came too late. I have already enlisted myself in that mighty army. You inquire if I am fond of poetry, I answer passionately, that is of a peculiar kind. The only poetry that I can read is Lord Byron. There is something so striking in his compositions, something so peculiarly beautiful that he fails not to engage the most of my attention and enlist my feelings. There seems to be nothing elaborate in his writing. In his "Childe Harold's Pilgrimage" we have the most intense imagery the loftiest sentiment and thought and the most extraordinary ease and harmony, one continued flow of his own native eloquence. "Manfred" is my favorite   I consider it his master piece   I never met with anything in my life so impressive as this   While reading it we seem to forget our relations to this world and are wafted to a land of Spirits. Reality recedes, and Fancy usurps her reign.

(April 3d)

I intended to have answered by this opportunity the numerous letters received from home through the kindness of William Carver, but being pressed for time I am obliged to defer it til another opportunity offers which will probably be in a few weeks, [The] brig "Bull" is trying to obtain a freight for New Bedford and will [pro]bably succeed. I was engaged at a large auction last Saturday, Monday and yesterday consequently my time has been nearly all occupied receiving and delivering goods.

The "Beer decoction" that father sent was received in good order. Beer is an article that is very little used here therfore I hardly think the demand for it would cover the expense of shipping it to these islands. Many thanks to John & Herbert for thier presents & kind letters I hope they will not fail to write by every chance that offers   I would write to them but I have no time. Also to Caroline and Edward tender to them my warmest thanks say to Caroline that I appreciate her good advise. I have a bone to pick with her. She accuses me of having no xxxxx indeed   She is much in fault for in the language of others I have one a *"big as a bushel basket."* The dickey that grandmother had the kindness to send me I am very much pleased with, it differs some in shape from those I am in the habit of wearing but I prefer the shape of this so much better that I shall have a lot made up like it immediately. I have not received a line from Aunt Cooper and but one letter from Sylvia since it pleased me to escape from the embrace of "Old Plymouth"   remember me to them most affectionately. John Vargue complains of my not writing, Say to him that I have received *one page* from him and have written him I believe *thirteen* in return. Remember me kindly to Mrs Sylvester, Sarah & Lydia and also present my dutiful respects to the "Old Colony Railroad." And now I charge you not to allow my friends to eulogise my letters to the extent you say they have done for if they do I shall forbid your showing them altogether, indeed they flatter me too warmly.

   Ever your Affectionate Brother James

       Honolulu November 3d 1845

My dear Sister

I have the pleasure to say that your kind letter pr Mindoro has been received not however until the vessel had been in port for three weeks, as the Capt of the Mindoro had a large invoice of goods on board it is supposed that he retained the letters for the purpose of selling his merchandise to a good advantage. We have every reason to believe that they were not held back by accident, consequently the indignant spirit of the community was aroused against him to the highest degree, he was shunned by all, no one would go to him to purchase, and finally was obliged to leave the port with most of his goods unsold. Such a malicious & unfeeling rascal deserves no pity.

Capt Dike has kindly offered to take home anything I may wish to send as presents. I therefore avail myself of the opportunity and his *good nature* and send a few articles that I have been able to collect amidst the hurry of business.   they are hardly worth the trouble of packing & sending them

You will please receive for yourself the fancy China Box, the perice of Ponga Silk and the trunk that contains the presents the peice of Silk I hardly know what you will do with. I do not fancy it as a dress   perhaps it will answer for curtains but however you use it in whatever way may please you, if at a loss I would suggest that it would make a magnificent *tunic* (I believe I have spelt it right) for Mother in law!!! I ommitted to say that one of the mantles are for you also.

Say to Caroline that my hurry will prevent me from writing to her by this conveyance in answer to her kind intentions to write by the Mindoro. With my warmest wishes hand her the following presents the Fancy China Box and one of the mantles.   by the next opp'y I will endeavour to send her something more worthy of her acceptance. I also send a Pocket knife for John, Herbert, & Edward which are valued here at $3.50¢ each, thus you see the econemy of sending presents home from this place they could probably be purchased at home for seventy five ct's or $1.—. Father will please accept the pair of Silver Suspender Buckles this is the most economical present I have sent they sell here for 7.$ & 8.$ Silver ware I believe is 25 or 30% more to the dollar at home than at this place. I have been looking but in vain for something suitible for my grandmother and Sylvia. I will endeavour to send them something when another opportunity offers

By the Mindoro I received but two letters yours and John's for which he will receive my warmest thanks. the Congarce [Congress] arrived here yesterday from Boston having left that port a few weeks after the Mondoro without bringing a *single letter.* what has induced my friends at home to desert me thus, is it because I do not write myself? perhaps it is. they are right. I appreciate their noble independence, but in the same word let me add that my feelings and affections are ever with them though mountains and oceans divide us, and if I do not favour them with a line I can assure them that it is not by any design of my own but only for want of time. While writing this I should in duty be engaged with my accounts

If I get time before Capt Dike sails I will endeavour to write a line to Father

Please Remember me to all my friends

Your Affectionate Brother
James

[pr "Chenamus"]

Honolulu   Oahu   Dec'r 20. 1845

My dear Sister

The "Chenamus" sails for the U. States this afternoon and being very much hurried at present with my accounts I shall not be able to write you so lengthy as

I would wish. I wrote you by Capt Dike a short time since which will in a measure excuse the briefness of this. The "Don Quixote" arrived here a few days since with a valuable cargo from the Coast. it is uncertain whether she will return again to the Coast or make a voyage to Valparaiso. Should she return to California I shall probably go the voyage in her to keep her accounts. I am anxious to take a sea voyage for a change. I am heartily tired of this confinement to the store. Moreover I think that I could do better with Uncle John than William for the latter is quick and passionate and the least trifling error on the part of those under his command calls forth a curse as for me I was not born to be forced. one kind word would go farther to call forth my energy and encourage me than the power of all the curses that were ever breathed Embodied in one word

You would be delighted to hear little Fanny prattle Spanish. She has grown stout and very pretty during her absence. John Henry is as usual full of *deviltry* and *fun* and the Charming little Nelly is in raptures by having her *old* playmates by her again. We have had an addition here lattly to our *countless* number of cousins a fine blue roguish eyed, good natured, smiling rascal, there is no name pinned on him yet. I presume he will be William Paty Jr.

Cannot stop to say more. – Remember me to all of my friends, and urge them to write.

In haste Your Affectionate Brother
James

Letters from Monterey
March to August 1846

[Care of John W. Sullivan Esq., Merchant, Boston]
Monterey, upper California
March 30. 1846
To Miss Frances A. Gleason, Plymouth
My dear Sister

The Don Quixote sails tomorrow morning for Mazatlan and I improve a few moments snatched from the hurry of my business to write you a few lines.

You will probably be somewhat surprised to hear from me about 2000 miles nearer my native home I arrived at this port on the 16th inst in the "Don Quixote" from the Sand'ch Islands I have been engaged on board the Bark keeping the accounts and have within a few days removed on shore to take charge, and dispose of the cargo brought from Oahu, an Invoice of about $8000. while the Bark is absent on the voyage to Mazatlan. The Don Quixote will return here probably in about three months and there is every prospect of making clear of all expenses the sum of 6000.$ She is chartered by the California Government to take two Commissioners down the Coast and return back immediately and is secured for the sum of 3000.$ cash but the most the Quixote will be benefitted by this charter will be on her return cargo

I was in hopes to have received letters from you before I left the islands. the Bark Angola arrived a few days previous to our departure having an extraordinary short passage of 117 days from Salem *no letters* there was also several vessels expected to arrive daily should they have letters on board for me they will probably remain at the Islands untill my return there which will probably be eight or ten months hence as it not frequently happens that vessels sail from the Islands to this place.   opportunities offer occassionally by vessels of war. I am much pleased with this coast, the climate is very healthy, and the Spanish lasses you are aware are so exceedingly amiable that one could almost imagine himself a portion of heaven while moveing through the dizzy waltz [1] with a beautiful blue eyed Spanish maid for a partner. But I have not time to enlarge on poetical ideas at present at some future time I may. To decend to a more serious and worldly subject I have to acquaint you of the loss of the ship "Fama" [2] on this coast a few weeks since   she was Commanded by Capt Nye (of Plymouth)   She went on shore in a gale of wind on the beach of Santa Barbary and will be a total loss   she had a cargo on board (mostly lumber) and was to sail in a few days for Oahu   the cargo will probably be all saved. At the time she was lost Capt Nye was on shore with his wife and the vessel was placed in charge of the mate (Mr

---

[1] The waltz was introduced in California in 1823 by some gay blades who arrived on the schooner *Rover* and, finding the fandango and jota not to their liking, taught the señoritas to dance the waltz. Soon the whole department was whirling to the time of 1-2-3, in close embrace. The padres appealed to Governor Argüello to pass a law prohibiting the new form of ecstasy but the governor was at the time too busy learning to waltz himself to bother with a new law.

[2] The American ship *Fama* was in Monterey when Commodore ap Catesby Jones arrived and the officers stated that reports of war between the United States and Mexico were current at Honolulu and that England had taken possession of California. These reports later proved to be unfounded.

Dunn) a man whose qualities as a seaman was placed in high estimation by those who were acquainted with him. I have written an account of this so that you can inform Capt Nye's friends of it in case they should not have heard of the loss. Capt Nye is now at St Barbary and is not aware of this opp'y to write home –

[The following letter, on the same letter sheets, is from Mary A. Paty to her niece Frances Gleason in Plymouth.]

On board Bark Don Quixote, Bay of Acapulco, April 10th/ 1846

My Dear Niece

James has left his letter unfinished for me to write a line in, and send it home by way of Mexico. but the Country is in such a state, I hardly think it practicable to send it at present, the report here is, that there is War between U. States and Mexico, and we expect it may be so. the male from Mexico has been due here, three weeks. they generally have one every week, [this] place is only three hundred miles from the City of Mexico, and [there] has been no communication for the last 20 days, and all are anxious to hear. this Vessel is Chartered by the California Government to take a commissioner to this place with dispatches for Mexico, he left here 15 days ago, we expect to hear from him this week when we shall know how much longer we have got to wait. we have been here 19 days to day, and we are all most eaten up by the musquetoes and it is the warmest place I was ever in and all together it is the most miserable. it is also subject to frequent earthquakes, there has been more than a dozen since we have been here, two or three quite heavy shocks I was quite alarmed, they caused such a noise on board — My little Fanny is almost sick with a cold, and my husband too, otherwise we are all well on board,— my poor little son I left at the Islands in a mission family. I am half inclined to go to the Islands in a Brig that is to leave for Oahu on Tuesday next (about 20 days passage)   John wants me to go, and to stay, so I do not know how it will be, he will deside to day. I have been with him so much he is quite lonely without me. — poor Sister Cooper and Caroline Augu[s]ta have met with a great loss and all of Mother Paty's family   I esteemed Mr Cooper very highly and am very [sor]ry he was cut off so suddenly, how important that we should always be prepared, as Death comes when we least expect it. I hope it may prove a blessing to some of us. — I wish you would write to me and write freely, — I know some of your little troubles and truly sympathise with you, but you must keep up good spirits and hope for better days, which I trust are in keeping for you.   please remember me kindly to your Father, and your Mother in law and to your brothers and to Edward Taylor. I have written to your Aunt Cooper, give my love to her to mother and Sylvia, tell Sylvia I shall write to her the first opportunity give my love to Uncle Thomas Paty's family   tell Aunt Maria I wish she would write to me, also remember me to Uncle E Paty and family and all Aunts and Uncles Cousins, and friends, Aunt Brewster Aunt Churchill, Mrs Rich and Mrs I Barnes and Mrs Southard Barnes — you requested me to send some of my hair which I will do with pleasure. I thank you all for the little presents you have sent, to Mother in particular I am very much obliged and Sylvia too, I will try and make some return to you all.

From Your Affectionate Aunt
Mary A. [Paty]

To Wm Paty Esq, Oahu [3]

Monterey April 5. 1846

dear Uncle

Mr Beldin leaves this place tomorrow for San Francisco and I have deemed it adviseble to leave a few lines with him in case some vessel should touch at that port bound for Oahu.

The Don Quixote sailed from this port yesterday bound to Acapulco San Blas and Mazatlan having been chartered by the California Government to take two Commissioners to the former place with the privilege of touching at the two latter to remain not exceeding fifteen days and is secured for the sum of $3000. cash.[4]

---

[3] All letters from April 5 through September 17, 1846 (except that for July 25) are transcribed not from originals but from Gleason's copy-book of his letters, including Ide's and Castro's proclamations, and Larkin's letter of May 4, 1846.

[4] The sailing captains took great pride in their vessels and were always ready for a trial of speed, the wager seldom being more daring than wine and cigars. The *Don Quixote,* though built before the days of the extreme clipper, nevertheless had a good turn of speed. In 1833, on a voyage from Callao to Honolulu, she averaged 200 miles a day for nearly the whole distance. On a round trip from Smyrna to Boston, she averaged nine knots an hour. In 1846 the run to Honolulu from Monterey was made in ten days.

In his diary, in 1842, Captain Paty notes, "We had a rather pleasant passage to Valparaiso, where we arrived in 97 days from Boston. The fast sailing ship *Congress,* left New York four days before us and arrived at Valparaiso eight days after us." This was the merchant ship *Congress,* carrying supplies to the missionaries at Oahu. Her captain, still smarting under his defeat, waited four days at Honolulu for the *Don Quixote* to be ready to leave, in order to have another trial. Both vessels set every sail, including stunsails, and for a time it looked like an even match. However, as night came on, the *Don Quixote* was well in the lead and the ships parted company, the *Congress* pointing her prow toward far distant China.

Again in 1842, the *Alert* and the *Don Quixote* were ready to leave Monterey at the same time and many wagers were made. Captain Paty found that his vessel trimmed too much by the head, and was not holding her own, so he had the crew shift all of the chain cable from the forward lockers and dragged to the after part of the bark. The *Don* slowly overtook her rival and by nightfall had fairly won the race.

In 1844, the *Don Quixote* raced the ship *Admittance,* a fast vessel of the Bryant & Sturgis Company. They left Santa Barbara for Monterey and it was a beat to windward all the way. Captain Peterson believed in keeping the

The Government have chartered the Don Quixote through Mr Tho's O. Larkin. I have enclosed you a copy of the contract which will inform you on the subject more plainly than I can write. Aside from this there is a contract with Don Jose Castro the Governor securing to Capt'n Paty the right of bringing a quantity of stores which will with an ordinary chance be a benefit to the concern of about $5000. it is also understood in the contract with the Governor that no tonnage dues shall be charged on the vessel either way

This charter happens very favourable as there can be nothing done on the coast in the way of making collections for the next two or three months and the Bark will return when the season for collecting commences. The cargo was all landed here from the Bark part of it has been sent to San Francisco to be disposed of by Mr Beldin who leaves tomorrow by land, and the remainder is placed in my charge to be sold at this place. I have a retail store fitted up and am instructed to sell only for immediate pay Mr Beldin has orders also to trust no person whatever.

We had a very quick passage here from the islands; we were but thirteen days from land to land we could have been at anchor here in fourteen days; we

---

Admittance far out to sea, while Captain Paty aimed to be near shore at sundown, to benefit by the night wind off the land. He brought the *Don Quixote* in to Monterey twenty-four hours ahead of the *Admittance!*

In the last days of Mexican rule in California, Governor Pío Pico preferred to reside in Los Angeles, so José Castro, Commandante Militar, took over civil authority at Monterey where he had possession of the customhouse and treasury. Another revolution was brewing and it was agreed to send Don Andréas Castillero and Ensign José Estrada to put the whole matter before the home government.

The *Don Quixote* was chartered to carry the commissioners to Mexico. After waiting at Mazatlan two weeks for the return of the commissioners and because war had broken out between Mexico and the United States, Captain Paty retraced his course to California.

Letters from Monterey, 1846

stood in and made the land off Monterey and squared away for San Pedro, on running down the coast we spoke the Vandalia and learned from her that it would be impossible for us to enter the cargo at San Pedro and concluded to alter our course for Monterey and were a week beating up the coast which made the passage twenty days from the islands.

Capt P. entered a cargo of about $5000. on which the duties amounted to $5200.   four months time, he has made sales to the amount of about $3000. most of it went towards off setting the duties.

I would write you more fully were I not so hurried at present in getting the San Francisco debts ready for Mr Beldin to collect   he is ready to go, and is waiting for me,

Please remember me to Cousin M.

Your Affectionate Nephew
Jas H. Gleason

To J. Beldin Esq., San Francisco
pr "Vandalia"   Monterey April 12, 1846
dear Sir

The Euphemia sales in a few days for San Francisco by her I shall send to you the San Francisco debts those that you now have are very imperfect as I have since learned by consulting Mr. Wm. Davis.

Should there offer an opportunity to communicate with the islands I think Capt Paty would be pleased to have you write to Mr. Wm. Paty at Oahu one of the firm of Paty & Co acquainting him of the arrival of the Don Quixote &c.

Yours Respectfully
Jas H. Gleason

To J. Beldin Esq., San Francisco
pr "Euphemia" Monterey April 15. 1846
dear Sir

Accompanying this I send you a book containing the San Francisco debts, the first page (John C. Davis account) you will see how I have arranged it. I have taken the amounts as t[hey] stand in the book and added to them the amount received since in goods which have not yet been copied in the books from the blotter of 1845 this being done I have subtracted the credits from the debits and to the balance added the balances of their accounts as they appear in the books of 1842.

Should you meet with any difficulty in settling up any of the accounts Mr. Wm. Davis will explain them to you if you ask him; he is of opinion that you can collect as well from the book which I send you as you can by the bills.

Mr. Thomas Cole has applied to me for $10.00 in goods $7.00 he says is for carting and the other $3.00 is for a spar which Capt Paty took with him to Mazatlan, he says that Capt Paty told you to pay him this amount please inform me if this is right by the earliest opportunity as I have declined paying the same untill I hear from you.

There is no news here of importance our friend Wigman is desperately in love with Jacoba I think he will get married soon.

Yours &c Jas H. Gleason

[To Capt. John Paty]
pr "Cyane" Monterey April 16. 1846
dear Uncle

The U.S. Ship Cyane arrived here this afternoon

having made a passage of twenty nine days from Oahu and sails tomorrow morning for Mazatlan which offers me an opportunity to send you a few lines.

Capt Mervine of the "Cyane" on leaving the islands gave word that he should sail direct for Mazatlan consequently she brings no letters. We learn however that the Brig Kamehameha III had arrived at Oahu having made the passage from the States in 120 days and that the Government were about purchasing her. It was reported also at the islands the new Commissioner was at the Society islands. The U.S. Ship "Congress" was at Oahu and was to sail shortly after the Cyane and as the latter had a long passage here she may be expected daily. I am in hopes to receive letters by her.

Business I am sorry to say is exceedingly dull the cash sales book shews an amount of only $120. since you left   every one says that trade was never known to be so dull before in Monterey. The piece of rainbow satin left with me I sold to Don Antonio Osio for $3.50¢ a vr* cash   he learned afterwards that you had sold some of the same for $2.50¢ vr which placed me in a rather unpleasant situation, but however I managed to smooth the affair over by a little equivocation and told him that if such was the case he should have it at the same price. Don Antonio is the only person in Monterey that I should have offered it to for sale. I offered him the refusal of it at first and wished to have it remain untill you should return but he told me not to be the least concerned about it   he would tell them that it was received as a present from Oahu.

The Euphemia sails tomorrow for [remaining part of the letter missing]

---
* Vara – a measurement, approximately a yard.

pr "Barnstable"   Monterey May 30, 1846
To Josiah Beldin Esq, San Francisco
dear Sir

Your favours of May 7, & 13th came duly to hand pr "Vandalia"

I send you herewith the blotter of 1845 agreeable to your wish.

I am pleased to learn that you have done so well with the invoice of merchandise placed in your hands. I have made sales to about $1000. of which $500. was cash and the balance sure pay which is much better than I anticipated when I first opened considering the great scarcity of money and the interference of two ("Euphemia" & "Barnstable's") well selected cargoes

I shall look for the "Don Quixote" at the latter part of this month when she will immediately proceed to San Francisco

I gave Mr Tooms the information you requested regarding the horse   I believe he is writing to you by this opportunity,

We have no news of importance.
                Yours &c   Ja's H. Gleason

---

pr "Angola"   Monterey June 13, 1846
To Wm Paty Esq., Honolulu
dear Uncle

The Angola leaves this port in a few days for Sitka and sails from thence to Oahu, Capt Varney tells me that he will not reach the islands untill the latter part of October or the first of November consequently it will not be of use to write much as an opportunity will offer soon by the Euphemia[5] which vessel is expected to

---

[5] The brig *Euphemia* was a former English bluff-bowed whaleship and though a dull sailer was a money maker for her owners. She was purchased

The Brig "Euphemia", a Pencil Sketch by Duncan Gleason
After the Gold Rush, many old ships were put to other uses.
The *Apollo* became a saloon, and the *Euphemia* served as a prison ship moored nearby.
Courtesy Devin Adair Co., publisher of Duncan Gleason's *Islands and Ports of California*

A Page from the Log Book of Captain John Paty
Commanding the schooner *Manuokawai*, Captain Paty annexed the two small islands of Laysan and Lisianski to the Hawaiian kingdom in the name of King Kamehameha IV.
Courtesy of The Public Archives, Honolulu

arrive here from the leeward about the first of July and proceed across the bay to Sta Cruz and take in lumber for the islands

Your favours pr Angola and Vancouver of dates April 28 & May 18th to Capt J. Paty were duly received and also my letters from the U. States which you were so kind to forward. I am pleased that you opened my letters from home   it was my intention to tell you to do so before I left the islands but I forgot it.

Capt Paty has now been absent 64 days   I shall look for him in about two weeks. Soon after he left the U.S. Ship Portsmouth arrived bringing us news that Mazatlan was on the point of being blockaded by the Americans   I thought at first that Capt Paty would meet with much difficulty but Mr Larkin a person concerned in the voyage gave me to believe that the difficulties in Mexico would not interfere with his voyage whatever.

I have made sales since the Don Quixote left to the

---

in 1845 by two brothers, Hiram and Eliab Grimes, and William Heath Davis, who acted as supercargo. She left the Hawaiian Islands in company with the *Don Quixote* in 1845 and sailed a losing race to the California coast.

Davis wrote, "Our brig had occasion to touch at a lower coast port before touching at Monterey." [Presumably to cache part of the cargo before declaring the remainder at the Monterey customs office!] At the latter port the customs officials requested to inspect the cargo which Davis readily agreed to, but remarked that there were many scorpions down below. His invoice was accepted *per se*. When the *Euphemia* sailed south she "took on board at a southern coast port an additional cargo of merchandise." [A proper smuggling operation!]

Sailing back to Monterey, Davis was surprised to find the Stars and Stripes floating from the customhouse staff. The *Euphemia* was the first vessel to enter the port after the American occupation and her cargo was much needed by the American warships.

During the Gold Rush, the brig with a gentle name was purchased by the administration to be used as a prison ship. When the sand hills of San Francisco were leveled and dumped into the bay, the old hulk was buried under sand lots so that in excavating for the Federal Bank Building at Sansome and Sacramento Streets in 1892, the steam shovel unearthed the timbers of the old vessel.

amount of about $1.100. Agreeable to Capt P's instructions when he left I have sold a little under the established price here for the object of realizing immediate pay. I received a line from Mr Beldin at San Francisco a few days since   he has sold about $2000. worth, when he left here I wrote a letter to you and placed it in his charge to be forwarded to Oahu by the earliest opportunity.   no chance has offered by last receipts. he must have arrived at San Francisco immediately after the Whaleship Valliant sailed

Mr McKinley has gone to Mexico and taken the Don Quixote Co's Books with him. it is probable that Capt. P. has met him in Mazatlan and made some arrangement with him regarding the accounts, he went with Mr Scott to purchase a cargo for this market   he is expected here daily.

Advises from the windward say that there has been much rain up the coast and the season provides well for collections.

June 15th

Since writing the foregoing the idea has occured to me that Capt Varney has no intention of going to Sitka but to proceed immediately to the islands   he has sold out his entire cargo here to Mr T. O. Larkin for   and received in exchange lumber and soap which he is now taking on board.   he is certainly aware of the demand for California lumber at the islands and should he go to Sitka the "Euphemia" will undoubtedly arrive at Oahu before him with her cargo which will greatly interfere with his sales. He met with some difficulty here with his cargo, the law obliges a person who anchors his vessel in this port to pay duties on his whole cargo.   this Capt Varney refused to do but consented to settle the tonnage dues (about $400.)

if this would be interesting to you I applied to Mr T. O. Larkin and he kindly loaned me his letter to the Secretary of State at Washington to copy from. you will find a copy of the same enclosed herewith

June 18

For the last few days there has been considerable excitement in this place   Dr Stokes arrived here from the upper Pueblo on Tuesday last bringing us intelligence that thirty seven americans had risen in the Sacramento and taken Sonoma [6] by force and made prisoners of four California officers & Don M. G. Vallejo Don Salvador Vallejo Don Victor Prudon and Mr Luis Leace   General Castro immediately mustered his forces in this place about 80 in number and this forenoon marched out to San Juan to arrange his troops and proceed to Sonoma to retake the place.   it is considered doubtful whether they will muster courage to meet them when they are prepared,

Evening

News has just reached us by a courier from Ludesdoff to Larkin confirming the report and furthermore states that the revolutioners show no flag and have issued a proclamation saying that they have made prisioners of the officers to further thier plans that they will be kindly treated and all property respected as long as no one molests them.   they have left twenty five men in Sonoma to guard the place and the remainder have gone on some other expedition. A man by the name of Ide said to be a very brave man is at the head of the "robbers" and it is supposed that Hastings is also concerned in it   a cabillado of about 150 horses was stolen a few days since by a branch of the same party,

---

[6] Sonoma is actually north of San Francisco, between Santa Rosa and Vallejo.

from some of General Castro's men whom he had sent to bring them to Monterey   it is beleived that the object of this is to take them into the mountains to meet the emigrants about 2000 in number now on thier way to this country. A revolution has now boldly commenced which will undoubtedly end very soon in an entire change of Government. This difficulty will greatly intefere with the traders in making collections this season.

Since writing the above a Proclamation has been received here which was issued by Mr Ide at the towns of Yerba Buena, Sonoma and the Pueblo (town) of San José. I have been able to take a copy of the same and enclose it herewith. We furthermore learn that his party has increased to about 60.   they have also hoisted a flag   it is white, with a red fly and a Star and a Bear in the union.

Mr Ide is said to be a man of about 40 years of age born in one of the Western States and came to California in September 1845   his family consists of a wife and five children now residing on the Sacramento River.

A Brig sailed a few days since for Mazatlan which carried the news of this revolution   as soon as it reaches Mexico she will evidently send on a large force to protect California.   should this so happen every foreigner on the coast will be obliged to join the "Bear" or leave the country.

I enclose you herewith a copy of the translation of General Castro's proclamation issued at this place.

I received a letter from Mr Beldin yesterday in which he says that there is great excitement in San Francisco and the revolution has prevented him from making any collections. The letter which I wrote to you and placed in his charge he forwarded by the H. B. Co Ship Columbia which vessel sailed about the 20th inst for Col'a [Columbia] River, remains a few days and proceeds to the islands.

Our last advises from the leeward report that Capt Nye is dangerously sick, we are expecting every day to hear news of his death.

The Euphemia is probably on her way now from San Pedro to this place.

I must close this for the present and send it on board for fear of losing the opportunity. If possible I will write more before the vessel sails

Please present my best regards to Cousin M. and the children and remember me to Von Pfisher

Your Affectionate Nephew
Ja's H. Gleason

Copy of Wm. B. Ide's Proclamation enclosed to Wm. P.[aty]

"A Proclamation to all persons and citizens of Sonoma requesting them to remain at peace and follow thier rights and ocupations without fear of molestation.

The Commander in Chief of the Troops assembled at the Fortress of Sonoma gives his inviolable pledge to all persons in California not found under arms that they shall not be disturbed in thier persons, thier property nor social relations one with another by men under his Command.

He also solemnly declares his object to be first to defend himself and companions in arms who were invited to this country by a promise of lands on which to settle themselves and families, who were also promised a Republican Government, when having arrived in California, were denied the privelege of buying or renting lands of thier friends, who instead of being allowed to participate in or protected by a Rep'can Government were oppressed by a military force of despotism, who were even threatened by proclamation by the chief officers of the aforesaid despotism with extermination if they should not depart out of the country leaving all thier property, arms and beasts of burden and thus deprived of the means of flight or defence we were to be driven through deserts inhabited by hostile Indians to certain destruction.

To overthrow a government who has seized upon the property of the Missions for its individual aggrandizement, which has ruined and shamefully oppressed the labouring people of California by thier enormous exactions on goods imported into this country is the determined purpose of the brave men who are associated under my command.

I also solemnly declare my object in the second place to be to invite all peaceable and good citizens of California who are friendly to the maintenance of good order & equal rights and I do hereby invite them to repair to my camp (without delay) to assist us in establishing and perpetuating a Republican Government which shall secure to us all civil and religious liberty, which shall encourage virtue & literature which shall leave unshackled by fetters Agriculture, Commerce, & Mechanism.

I further declare that I rely upon the rectitude of our intentions, the favour of Heaven and the bravery of those who are bound to and associated with me by the principles of self-preservation, by the love of truth and the hatred of tyranny for my hopes of success.

I furthermore declare that I believe that a Government to be prosperous and happy must originate with the people who are friendly to its existance, that the citizens are its guardians, the officers its servants, and its glory its reward,

(Signed) William B. Ide

Head quarters Sonoma
June 18, 1846

Translation of Gen'l Castro's Proclamations

The citizen José Castro Lieutenant Colonel of Horse in the Mexican Army and acting General Commandante of the Department of California.

Fellow citizens, the low policy of the agents of the U. States of the north in this department have got up a portion of adventurers that boldly and without respecting the rights of men have began to invade it, having taken possession of the town of Sonoma sur-

Letters from Monterey, 1846

prising the military commander of that frontier Colonel M. G. Vallejo Lieut Col. Don Victor Prudon Captain Don Salvador Vallejo & Mr Jacob P. Leace.

Fellow countrymen the defence of our liberty, the true religion professed by our fathers and our independence obliges us to sacrafice ourselves, rather than lose these inestimable blessings, banish from your hearts all low ideas of resentment turn you faces, open your eyes and behold these families and innocent children which have unfortunately fallen into the hands of our enemies, snatched from the bosom of thier fathers who are now prisoners among the foreigners and calling loudly on us for assistance. It is yet time for us to form one solid mass which shall be impregnable and full of justice.   doubt not but the Divine providence will dictate to us the way to glory & at the same time you ought not for one moment to doubt that in this General quarters notwithstanding the smallness of the garrison of which it is composed that the very first who sacrafices himself will be your fellow citizen and Friend,
(Signed) José Castro

Head quarters Santa Clara
June 17th 1846
And that this may reach the notice of all persons, I command that it be published and circulated and fixed in the customary conspicuous places   (Signed) J. S. Escamilla
Alcalde

The citizen José Castro Lieutenant Colonel of Horse in the Mexican army and acting General Commandant of the Department of Upper California,

All the foreigners pacifically residing amongst us occupied in thier business may rest assured of the protection of all the authorities of the Department always admitting that they mix in no revolutionary movements. The General Commandancia under my charge will never lightly proceed against any person whatever, niether will it be carried away by mere words wanting proof to support them, there shall proper declarations be taken proofs exacted and the liberties and rights of the laborious which is always commendable shall be protected.

Let the fortune of war take its chance with those ungrateful persons who with arms in thier hands have attacked the country without remembering that at some former time they were treated by him who subscribes with all that indulgence of which he is characteristic. The impartial inhabitants of the Department are witnesses to the truth of this. I have nothing to fear, my duty must conduct me to death, or victory. I am a MEXICAN SOLDIER and I will be free and independent or die with pleasure for these inestimable blessings.

(Signed) José Castro

Head quarters Santa Clara
June 17, 1846

And that this may reach the notice of all I command that it be published and circulated and posted in the customary conspicuous places

(Signed) Joaquin Escamilla
Alcalde of Monterey

Copy of Mr T. O. Larkin's letter to the Secretary of State at Washington respecting the mines of California enclosed to Wm Paty Honolulu S. I.

May 4, 1846

The undersigned has the honor to forward to the Department the following information respecting the mines of California most of them discovered within six or nine months, for many years previous to this the inhabitants have supposed the places in question contained metal of some kind. (90 miles by sea) South of San Diego there are some very extensive copper mines belonging to Don Juan Bandine.

The undersigned is informed by Don Jose Rafael Gonsales that on his ranch 60 or 80 miles south of Monterey there are coal mines, at San Pablo (in the bay of San Francisco) there are others. At the Mission of San Juan 25 miles north of Monterey there are sulphur beds or mines. 50 to 80 miles north of Monterey there is said to be several silver mines. There are several places throughout Calif'a where the people obtain a betuminous pitch to cover the roofs of their houses, some make a floor of it by mixing earth with it at these places rabbits, squirrels & birds often get half burried in the pitch and soon die even horses & horned cattle are lost there. A few miles north of St'a Barbary the sea for several miles upon the coast is coloured by the pitch ouzing from the banks. 5 or 6 miles from the town of San José & near the Mission of St'a Clara there is a mountain of quick silver ore discovered by Don Andres Castillero (of Mexico) in 1845 which the undersigned has twice seen produce 20 pr ct. of pure quick silver by simply putting the pounded rock in an old gun barrel one end placed in the fire and the other in a pot of water for the vapour to fall into which immediately becomes condensed   the metal was then strained through a silk hkf – the red ore produces far better than the yellow. – there appears no end to the production of the metal from the mountain – Working of the quick silver has but now commenced under great disadvantages from not having any of the materials generally used in extracting that metal. Near the town of Sonoma about 60 miles from the entrance to the Bay of San Francisco there are other mines the rock or ore of which appears of a grayish cast & said to be equal to the others. Near the same town there are Sulphur mines, the peice the undersigned has in his possession is perfectly pure without rock or dirt mixed with it. At the same place is said to be lead mines, some indians have brought a blanket full of lead ore to the Mission of San Juan refusing to tell from whence they brought it. On the ranch of Capt Richardson one side of the entrance to the Bay of San Francisco there is a lead mine, the undersigned has 2 or 3 pounds said to be from that rancho.   this is full of peble stones which when taken out by a nail or knife left the lead entirely pure and indented similar to honey comb.   20 miles from Monterey there is a mine of silver & lead which has been taken out but not extracted.   there is also much slate of the best quality at the Sacramento River. There is said to be black lead in the country. At San Fernando near San Pedro by washing the sand in a plate any person can obtain from 1. to 5.$ pr day of gold that brings 17.$ pr oz in Boston   the gold has been gathered for 2 or 3 years though but few have patience to look for it.

On the Southeast end of the island of Catalina there is a silver mine from which silver has been extracted   there is no doubt but that gold, silver, quick silver, copper lead, sulphur & coal mines are to be found all over Calif'a & it is equally doubtful whether under thier present owners they will ever be worked.   the Indians have always said there was mines in the country but would not show thier location & the Calif'ans did not choose to look for them. By the laws & customs of Mexico respecting mining every person or Co. foreign or native can present themselves to the nearest authorities & denounce any unworked mine. the authorities will then after the proper formalities put the denouncer in possession of a certain part or all of it according to the extent of the mine   the possessor must hereafter occupy and work this mine or some other person may denounce against him. In all cases the Gov'mt claims a certain portion of the products. Up to the present time the[re] are few or no persons in California with sufficient energy & capital to carry on mining. A mexican officer of the army, a Padre and a native of New York are on a very small scale extracting quick silver from the San José mines.

          I Remain &c
          [Thomas O. Larkin]

---

pr. "Angola"   Monterey June 25, 1846
To R. G. Davis* Esq., Honolulu
dear Sir

 Your brother when he left this place requested me to send you a few lines should an opportunity offer to communicate with the islands.

 The "Moscow" arrived here a few days since from the leward. Mr Robinson the clerk tells me that he saw Mr Davis at San Pedro and appeared to be doing well with his cargo, but did not learn what amt. he had sold, he was to sail in a few days for this port; on his arrival here he will (as he gave me to understand when he left) go to Santa Cruz and load with lumber for the islands, he will probably take on board some soap at the leward. I believe that it is the intention of your brother to remain on the coast to collect while the brig is absent on her voyage to Oahu.

 A revolution has now commenced here which it is feared will cause considerable trouble in Calif'a for

---
* A brother of William Heath Davis.

Letters from Monterey, 1846 111

some years. Mr Wm. B. Ide said to be an active energetic & well informed man with a party of about 60 americans under his command took possession of Sonoma a few days since & made prisoners of Don M. G. Vallejo military commandant of Sonoma, Don Salvador Vallejo, Mr Luis Leace & Don Victor Prudon. the latter was Captn & Secretary. These prisoners are now on Feather River a branch of the Sacramento held as supposed as hostages to enable thier capturers to further thier designs. About thirty of thier party remain in charge of Sonoma. They have to this time respected all property with the exception of taking about 150 horses belonging to the California Government, it is supposed that they have seized these horses to take into the mountains to meet a large party of emigrants which are soon expected.

General Castro now remains at Santa Clara with about 200 men under his Command, it is considered doubtful whether Castro will go north to meet the "Bear".

Mr Ide and his party, have a white flag, red fly and with one star and a bear in the union,[7]

---

[7] In the exciting year of 1846 rumors were rife that General Castro planned to liquidate the American settlers in California, so a company led by William B. Ide decided to set up an independent territory and, raising a flag with a crude replica of a bear, loudly proclaimed the California Republic.

They occupied the town of Sonoma and took Don Mariano Vallejo a prisoner. Vallejo was a staunch supporter of American interests and Thomas Larkin had relied upon him to bring about the peaceful annexation of California by the United States government. This episode upset his plans. Vallejo was taken to Sutter's Fort and held a captive for two months despite the protests of Sutter.

At this time Captain John Charles Frémont arrived in California. He headed an exploring expedition sponsored by the United States Topographical Engineers. The party, which included a botanist, a topographer and an artist, reached the Columbia River, turned south and after much hardship arrived at Sutter's Fort. Leaving one of his men (Edward Kern for whom the Kern River was named) in charge of prisoners, he gave instructions, "Iron and

Remember me to Webster and say that I have not time to write to him.

       Yours truly
        Ja's H. Gleason

[Per bark Angola, Capt S. Varney]
To Wm Paty Esq., Oahu   Monterey July 3d, 1846
dear Uncle

Capt Varney tell me that he sails this afternoon direct for Oahu.

Several of General Castro's party arrived in town last evening and report that a party of sixty Californians under the command of Gabriel de la Torre while marching towards Sonoma suddenly came upon a party

---

confine any person who shall disobey your orders – if necessary shoot any person who shall endanger the safety of the place."

 Archibald H. Gillespie, Lieutenant of the United States Marine Corps, chose a dangerous route through a country on the verge of war with his own. Reaching the Pacific shore at Mazatlán, the U.S. Sloop-of-war, *Cyane* carried him to Monterey where he gave a secret message to Larkin and then set out to find Frémont. The trail was picked up at Sutter's Fort and two trappers joined him in his search through a trackless territory filled with hostile Indians. As the trail became hot, one of the guides sped on ahead and found Frémont who turned back with him. Gillespie and Frémont met on May 9, 1846, just when the Mexican War started on the Rio Grande.

 That night as the men lay sleeping a hail of arrows announced a midnight attack by the Klamath Indians. A desperate fight ensued and the Indians were driven off, but three of their arrows had found a deadly mark. A punitive expedition set out and after two days the band was overtaken and paid dearly for this treachery.

 Gillespie's message to Frémont and Larkin was likely an enjoinder to win the friendship of the Californians and gradually wean them over to the United States. Frémont therefore took no active part in the revolt, but nevertheless accepted the custody of the prisoners at Sutter's Fort. In other ways Frémont found it difficult to keep his fiery patriotism in check. When Captain de la Torre advanced to retake Sonora, Frémont's forces drove the Mexicans back to the shore and into their boats. The American bark *Moscow* was at Sausalito and Captain Phelps supplied boats to Frémont, who chased the Californians across the bay. Frémont found the guns at Fort Point deserted so he spiked them by driving files, secured from the *Moscow,* into the priming holes, rendering them useless.

of about 300 americans on the road near Sonoma. Each party fired once and retreated ten Californians were killed and on the other side one american and one frenchman. the americans were a scouting party sent out by Ide, as soon as they fired they hastened with speed to the camp to put them on the guard. Ide immediately collected his men 150 in number, Castro's men about 160 soon made thier appearance on the opposite side of the river but finding the american party so strong in numbers they dared not attempt an engagement, they all retreated to head quarters Santa Clara where they now remain. it is generally supposed here that Castro is now defeated, his men are all deserting him he had at first 200 now he can only number about 160.

The U.S. Ship "Portsmouth" is now lying at Saucalito and supplies in a secret manner Ide's party with provisions and ammunition. It is generally believed here that Capt Fremont is the mover of this revolution. Gillespie arrived here a short time since as bearer of despatches to Fremont on his arrival he found that Fremont had purchased horses and provisions and had been absent eight days on the road to Oregon, Gelespie travelled day and night untill he came up with him. he overtook him about 500 miles from the place he started from. Fremont immediately returned with his party and camped near Sonoma and soon commenced the revolution.

Last evening we expected to have a hot skirmish in this place, it seems that a Californian being a friend to the americans, informed Mr Larkin the american Consul that a secret meeting was to be held that night among the authorities of the place to see whether it would be adviseable to seize him prisoner, about twilight he [Larkin] sent round word to his friends to have thier fire arms ready for immediate use, and should there be a report of fire arms in the night to hurry to his house it seems that the Californians did not deem it prudent to make the attack. it is supposed that they wish to make prisoner of Larkin to influence the release of the prisoners in possession of Ide.

We have in port the U.S. Ships "Cyanne", "Levant" and "Savannah" the latter arrived on Tuesday last twenty two days from Mazatlan. The Don Quixote had not arrived at that port when she left. The "Juanita" sailed six days previous to the "Savannah" for this place and has not yet arrived,

Capt Hinkley died a few days since in Yerba Buena.

Mr Wm Hartnell wishes you to get a watch from Mr Boardman taken to the Islands to be repaired by Capt Nye and whatever charges there may be on the same settle for and he will make it good to Capt Paty. he wishes you to send it to him by the earliest opportunity with a bill of expenses.

I have not time to write more as the vessel is ready for sea.

Please remember me to all friends   In haste
Your Affectionate Nephew
Ja's H. Gleason

To R. C. Wyllie Esq.   Monterey July 3d 1846
H. H. M. Secretary of State
  For Foreign Affairs &c &c &c
dear Sir

The Barque Don Quixote is now absent on a voyage to Mexico. Capt Paty when he left wished me to write to you should an opportunity offer to communicate with the Islands during his absence.

For the last few weeks there has been great excitement on this Coast. Early in the morning of June 14th a party of about thirty four americans headed by a person named Ide, rose in Sonoma, took possession of the place without meeting with any oposition on the part of the Californians and made prisoners of Colonel M. G. Vallejo, Lieut. Colonel Don Victor Prudon, Captain Don Salvador Vallejo & Mr I. P. Leace. As soon as the news reached this place Don Juan Baptista Alvarado mustered about eighty men and proceeded to Santa Clara to join General Castro. the Californians mustered about 400 strong General Castro placed fifty men under command of Joaquin de la Torre, fifty under Jose Antonio Carrillo, and fifty under Francisco Rico and marched towards Sonoma to retake the place.

I received a letter this morning from a person residing at San Francisco dated June 29th which is the latest news received here. He gives me the following information. Mr Ide's party has increased to about 200 men, half of them are at San Rafael and the others remain at the Mission of Sonoma with both places well fortified. The party of Californians under Command of Joaquin de la Torre while marching towards Sonoma on the morning of the 28th of June met a party of Ide's men twelve in number each party fired once and immediately retreated on the Californians side three were killed and five wounded on the other side one frenchman and one american was killed, A party of about 130 men under command of General Castro was seen on the 28th of June on the point of San Pablo opposite San Rafael waiting to cross the river the foreigners on the Sonoma side intend to let Castro pass over with all his force and then rush upon them. We are anxiously waiting now to hear the result of this engagement. Nearly all the families on the Sonoma side have gone down to Mr. Richardson's house for protection.

It is reported here that the Californians took two foreigners prisoners on the road and barbourously murdered them, and in return the american party shot three Californians, couriers from Jose Antonio Carrillo to General Castro, one of them was Manuel Castro, brother in law to the General,

We have now lying in this port the U.S. Ships "Savannah", "Levant" and "Cyanne" the former arrived on Tuesday last twenty two days from Mazatlan, she brings no news. She sails next week for San Francisco. The U.S. Ship "Portsmouth" is at Saucalito and the English Sloop of war "Juno" is lying at San Francisco.

I have the honor to subscribe myself
Your most Obedient Servant,
Ja's H. Gleason

[pr "Collingwood"   Monterey U.S. of America
To Wm Paty Esq., Honolulu]   July 23d 1846
dear Uncle

Mr Hencley the first Lieutenant of the "Collingwood" has just called at my room   he tells me that it is not known whether the Collingwood goes to Oahu or not but has kindly offered to take a letter to said place for me and should she not go there he will tear it up.

Commodore Sloat took possession of this place on the 7th inst.   a courier was immediately sent by the Commodore to San Francisco with orders to Captain Montgomery of the Portsmouth to hoist the flag of the United States at that place   we are now on american soil and it is generally believed that the flag will never be lowered again   had I time I would forward you

The Flag of
Los Estados Unidos
Mejicanos, 1825

The First Bear Flag
1846

The American Flag
28 Stars – 1846

The Old Customhouse at Monterey
From the sketchbook of Duncan Gleason

THE HOME OF GOVERNOR ALVARADO AT MONTEREY
This property later belonged to James Henry Gleason.

Commodore Sloat's Proclamation. I presume that the Admiral will take it if he goes to the Islands. American goods are now imported here duty free and foreign goods one quarter what they paid heretofore. a vessel from the states or from the Islands with a cargo of Provisions would pay well — The Squadron has thrown a great deal of money into this place they have established a company of horse called the California Dragoons commanded by Purser Fontleroy of the "Savannah" thier object is to go up and down the coast to protect the people from being molested by the Indians.

Captain Fremont arv'd here last Sunday with a party of 170 riflemen under his command he is now camped about quarter of a mile from town. it is supposed that his next movement will be to go to the leward to take Castro and bring him to this place. If this can be effected the people of the country will go quietly about thier ocupations and trade will again revive [8]

---

[8] War was declared with Mexico in May 1846, but news of the event did not reach the Pacific Coast until August 12th. In the meantime Commodore John D. Sloat lay at Mazatlán with the U.S. Frigate *Savannah* and the Sloops-of-war *Portsmouth* and *Cyane,* watching the movements of *H.M.S. Collingwood.* Thomas Larkin, the American consul at Monterey, sent word to Sloat urging that warships were needed for the protection of American citizens. The *Portsmouth* was dispatched to Sausalito and the *Cyane* to Monterey. Sloat, upon receipt of unofficial word that war had been declared with Mexico, left Mazatlán with all sail set alow and aloft, fearing that the British ship *Collingwood* was close on his wake.

Arriving at Monterey he was in a quandary as no war news had reached the coast and he did not want to repeat the fiasco of Commodore ap Catesby Jones. The Fourth of July was celebrated on board the gaily dressed ships, with band concerts. On the sixth however, a council of war was held and the following day a company of marines was landed under command of Captain William Mervine of the *Cyane.* They marched up to the customhouse and hoisted the American ensign without opposition. A whaleboat propelled by oars and sail was dispatched to Yerba Buena and also a courier on a swift California horse galloped by land to reach the *Portsmouth* first with orders to

The Euphemia sailed a few days since for San Fran-

Captain Montgomery to take possession of Yerba Buena. The *Portsmouth* moved over to the pueblo and a company of seventy marines was put ashore. As was done in Monterey, they marched up to the Plaza in step to the martial music of fife and drum and, encountering no opposition, the Mexican flag was lowered and the Stars and Stripes hoisted. The Plaza was renamed Portsmouth Square.

Washington A. Bartlett, Lieutenant of the *Portsmouth,* was made Alcalde of Yerba Buena and on January 9, 1847, by decree, changed the name of the pueblo to San Francisco.

General Stephen W. Kearny had been sent west to take possession of Arizona, New Mexico and, as he thought, of the western seaboard. But California's destiny had always been linked with ships and it was with some chagrin that Kearny heard that a goodly fleet of men-o'-war had accomplished what he had traveled so many miles to do.

Kit Carson, whom he had met on the trail on his way to Washington, had reported that all was serene and peaceful when he left Los Angeles, so Kearny left part of his forces at Santa Fe to uphold the flag. Sending another courier on to Washington with Carson's dispatches, Kearny then set out for California. Robert Stockton learned of the approach of the remaining force of General Kearny and sent Captain Gillespie with twenty men to warn him of the hostile state of the country and to caution him against a conflict.

On the other hand, Kit Carson had assured Kearny that the Californians were cowards and would not stand to fight. The company now numbered 161 men but their mounts, mostly mules, were worn out after the long journey. Riding along the bed of the San Bernardino River, a few miles east of present Escondido, the vanguard under command of Captain Johnson, came suddenly upon a force of eighty Californians, led by Andrés Pico.

With a yell, the Americans dashed forward, only to fall back with their captain dead and several men wounded. Fifty dragoons under Captain Moore came up and charged at the Californians who fled at first but, suddenly wheeling about, came back with such vigor that the Americans were thrown into confusion. The worn out horses and mules stampeded as the Californians charged with their lances, weapons about eight feet long and tipped with a sharp metal blade, which did deadly work. Captain Moore was killed and both Kearny and Gillespie were wounded.

The Americans retreated west to the Escondido mountains, where they entrenched themselves at a point now known as "Starvation Peak" or "Mule Hill." Kearny's dead numbered some 25 and many wounded. Considering the small number of United States forces engaged, this was one of the most deadly battles ever fought by American troops.

Food and water were running low but the Americans were afraid to stir from their position, so Kit Carson and Lieutenant Beale slipped through the enemy's lines during the night and made their way to San Diego. Two hundred marines were hurried to the relief and with this escort the beleaguered army arrived safely at San Diego, with a high regard for the fighting qualities of the Californians.

cisco, she will leave this place about Aug 1st for the islands. Capt Nye takes passage in her.

I have made sales to date since the Quixote left about 1600.$, $950, cash remainder hides & tallow.

The U.S. Ship Congress arrived here a few days since from Oahu   I have not heard any news whatever   she brought letters from C. Brewer & Co. to Mr Howard but he is up the coast.

Mr Hencley has called to take this and I must close.
In haste   Your Aff. Nephew
J. H. Gleason

[pr "Collingwood"]   Monterey July 23d 1846
To Wm Paty Esq., Honolulu
dear Uncle

It has just been made public that the Collingwood frigate leaves this place in about two hours for the Islands consequently I have but time to write a few lines.   her topsails are now already loosed.

The Collingwood arrived at this port about a week since from San Blas making the passage in thirty one days   she left the Don Quixote off Cape St Lucas about fifty miles to the leward   she ought to have arrived here before this. I am inclined to think that she has touched in at San Pedro to bring up some agaudiente. I am exceedingly anxious for her to arrive as there is a probability of Commodore Sloat chartering her to go to the Islands to bring on provisions for the Squadron.   the commodore thought of chartering the "Euphemia." I believe the reason he did not was that she was too small.

No more time is allowed me to write — in haste
Your Affectionate Nephew
Ja's H. Gleason

[Cover: Miss Frances A. Gleason
            Plymouth, Mass, U. States of America
From Paty & Co.
Care of J. W. Sullivan Esq., Merchant, Boston
Forwarded by John W. Sullivan, Boston, Aug. 17/47]
[Postmarked: New York, Aug. 16, 7cts;
    Boston, Aug. 17, 5 cts — 13 months in transit]

Monterey   U. *States of America*
July 25, 1846

My dear Sister

My last to you was sent by the "Don Quixote" bound to Mazatlan which was to be forwarded across Mexico; and on account of the troubles between Mexico and the United States I am inclined to think it will never reach you, I arrived on this coast in March last in the "Don Quixote", immediately on the arrival of the Bark she was chartered by the Californian Government to take a commisioner to Mazatlan and her cargo was landed here and placed in my charge to dispose of which I have nearly sold out. I am now looking for the arrival of the Bark every hour   the English frigate "Collingwood" arrived here a few days since from San Blas she saw the Quixote off Cape St Lucas bound for this port. This will reach you at the same time the news reaches the United States that the territory of California is another star in our union. Commander Sloat landed a force at this place of about three hundred men marines and sailors from the squadron in the harbour on the 7th inst. and hoisted the flag of the United States. I[t] seems exceedingly pleasant to me to place my feet once more on american soil. Should the flag continue to wave here there will be fine prospects for young persons just commencing life   I have already purchased a house lot immediately in the centre of this town and I expect to be in San Francisco in two or three weeks when I shall buy me a farm on the Sacremento River. land can be purchased at the present time very cheap as soon as news reaches the U.S. that this country is in possession of americans, emigration will rush here in thousands and make lots immensely valuable. I once thought that the Sandwich Islands was a delightful place but now give me California with its beautiful sky and its lovely señoritas they have given me a name here of Patito chicita (little Paty) because I look so much like Uncle John. I shall never go to the Islands again to live. It is possible I may go soon on a visit, in future you can send letters to me by vessels bound to this coast and also by vessels bound to the Islands from which place they will always be forwarded to me.

You are very anxious for me to come home. I believe you dear Sister, but why destroy the fine prospects that are now presented to me by being absent eighteen months or two years on a voyage home every month so absent would be a sacrafice to me of at least $200. what would be my chance of becoming wealthy in Plymouth I can see none, but here there is a prospect. I am received into the highest society and *respected far more than I would be at home*.[9]

[The greater likelihood is that I shall go as a *married* man. Do not spread your eyes at the hint for to be honest about it I am engaged to the Belle of Monterey! Miss Kate Watson. They are fine people all of them and my Kate is beyond compare. Her father James Watson is a great honest hearted man who is a friend to every one. He is quite well off being worth about

---

[9] Six lines are here missing from the original letter. The four paragraphs in brackets are inserted from Gleason's copy book of letters, which paragraphs seem not to be in the original letter.

60,000$. He is very hospitable and his house at the rancho near town is the stopping place for all his friends.]

[I received a few days ago several letters from Plymouth. Yours I read with tears in my eyes your unhappiness gives me great pain.]

[I am very much hurried in getting my accounts settled for the arrival of the "Don Quixote." The "Levant" sails today under command of Commodore Page. Commodore Sloat returns by her to the U. States he will be greatly missed here. He is held in the highest esteem not only by our citizens but by being a worthy man and an able commander, he has the confidence and respect of his squadron and officers for his actions here posterity will revere and honor him.]

[You can hardly imagine the confusion into which our country has been thrown by this revolution though this state of affairs will probably be of short duration if Colonel Fremont is successful in his southern expedition. he sailed two days ago in the Cyane for San Diego there they are to secure horses and advance upon Castro at Los Angeles.]

. . . when the Quixote arrives I shall try to make some arrangement with Aunt Mary Ann (who is now absent in her) to have you come out here, you will certainly be more comfortable with me than at home. How my *sweet Katarina* and you would love each other. I little thought when I left home that I should unite my fortunes with a Spanish maiden. I have not as yet but my friends say that I am desperately near it.

You must excuse me for bringing my letter to a close so soon as I am very much hurried at present in getting my accounts ready for the arrival of the "Don Quixote." I send this by the U.S. Ship "Levant" in charge of Lieut. Hamsley who has kindly offered to forward it across Panama, it will rea[ch] you soon

Please give my love to John and Herbert Grandmother, Aunt Cooper, Caroline & Edward Sylvia &c. &c.

In haste   Your dear Brother
James

To Capt John Paty
Monterey   U.S.A.   July 30, 1846
dear Uncle

The great improbability of this not meeting you in San Pedro will prevent me from writing much.

The "Barnstable", "Moscow", "Sterling", "Tasso", "Vandalia" and "Euphemia" are now lying at San Francisco.

Advises from that place say that there will be few collections this season owing to the disturbances in the country. It is hoped that Capt Fremont with his party (who is now on his way to the leward) will take Castro. The people of the country would return quietly to thier homes and trade will again revive.

I am exceedingly anxious for your return as business is very dull here.

I have made sales since your departure from this place to the amount of about $1,700.   over $1,000. cash.

In haste   Your Affectionate Nephew
Ja's H. Gleason

To J. Beldin Esq., Yerba Buena
Monterey   Aug 2. 1846
dear Sir:

I enclose you herewith a list of merchandise which I shall forward you by the "Tasso" which vessel sails tomorrow for your place. I shall also send the Kanaka which I have with me agreeable to your wish   it is impossible to hire men here at present unless at an extravagant price. With regard to what goods you now have on hand, I think that in order to hurry them off you had better dispose of them on credit to persons that you know have ranches and take thier notes payable at a given time, for the same as goods are now falling in price every day and should this territory continue to be a portion of the United States and a well organized Government established the notes will evidently be good.

A courrier arrived last evening from the leward and reports that the Don Quixote arrived at San Pedro seven days since. I shall look for her here by day after tomorrow.

In haste   Your Obedient Servant
Ja's H. Gleason

To J. Beldin Esq., Yerba Buena

                        Monterey August 3d 1846

dear Sir

I have shipped on board the "Tasso" to your charge the following merchandise

    1 case marked y D #8251 containing:

12 ps Prints (assorted)	6 gro Bone Buttons
4 ps Wide Silk	1 Box Night Caps
12 Fancy " Handkfs/small	Lot Needles
3 ps " – " " /large	3 doz Elastic Garters
10 " " Blk" "	3 vests
3 " Corded Muslin	4 ps Cambric
6 " Mull "	6 " Toweling
2 " Narrow Silk	1 " Silk & Cotton
4 doz Childrens Stockings	6 Neck Stocks
1 Box Spool Cotton	6 ps Wht. Cotton
1 " Ball "	1 Sword Belt
6 ls Linen thread	2 Camphor Cloaks

Letters from Monterey, 1846

2 " Blue Cotton "	1 Box Narrow Ribbons
2 " Wht. " "	12 Gro. Fish Hooks
1 doz Spool " "	12 " Cut Tacks
2 ls Blk Sewing Silk	1 Bag Shot
3 gro Metal Buttons	1 doz Blacking

also

1 Case mark'd P #4 Cont'g
  20 ps Prints (Assorted)   4 ps Blue Cotton
  6 " Narrow Bro. Cottons

I have just finished a letter to you and sent it by Mr Toomes to San Juan to be forwarded when an opportunity offers and as it is probable that this will reach you first it will not be amiss to mention again that it was Captain Paty's instruction to us when he left to sell to those persons only who you felt sure would pay this season but as circumstances have so materially changed within a few weeks, I think it best to get the goods off our hands as soon as possible. If no other way you had better sell to persons who hold property and take thier notes for the same payable at some specified time: and if we have well established laws here as it appears we soon shall have the purchasers will be obliged to meet the notes or become insolvent and forfiet thier lands. Business is exceedingly dull at this place. I have only sold about $1800 worth, had I gone to the leward instead of remaining here I could have sold out everything for pay down.

The Don Quixote arrived at San Pedro last Monday. I shall look for her here in a few days.   on her arrival we shall use every exertion to get up to Yerba Buena.

I have sent my Kanaka to you by the "Tasso."

There is no news here of importance. I learn that Castro is at the leward with 800 men under his command.   Your Obedient Servant
                                Ja's H. Gleason

[pr "Euphemia" Monterey Aug 22nd 1846
To Wm Paty Esq., Oahu]
dear Uncle

The Brig Euphemia sails tomorrow for the Islands and I improve the opportunity to send you a few lines.

I was in hopes that the Don Quixote would have arrived here ere this so that I could have been able to give you some information respecting his voyage to Mexico also some definite idea of Capt Paty's future movements. On his arrival here I presume he will make every exertion possible to get up to San Francisco. Mr Davis [10] informs me that not one Californian has made a matanzas [slaughter] this season.   up the coast but there are many hides in circulation which Capt. Paty will be likely to obtain when he arrives there.

The Don Quixote will have been on the coast four weeks day after tomorrow. She arrived first at San Pedro. the last intelligence I have from her I received last night by a Government Courrier three days from Santa Barbary, a person writes that that Bark left that port "a few days since" bound to this place. Consequently I am looking for her every hour, I am inclined to think that she will touch in at St Luis Obispo on her way up, if so, she will not be here for several days yet.

---

[10] William Heath Davis, born in Honolulu in 1822, was the son of William Heath Davis Sr., a trader and one time governor of Oahu. His mother, Hannah, was the daughter of Oliver Holmes whose wife was a pure-blood Polynesian.

He first visited California as a boy of nine and again at the age of eleven. In 1838, when sixteen years old, he arrived on the *Don Quixote* and was employed by his uncle, Nathan Spear, as clerk in Spear's store at Monterey. When Spear moved to Yerba Buena, Davis accompanied him. After four years he started out for himself, to become one of the leading merchants and ship owners of Yerba Buena, later called San Francisco.

In 1847 he married María de Jesús, daughter of Don Joaquin Estudillo, a prosperous cattle rancher. Davis did much to guide the city from a small pueblo to a great metropolis. (Davis, *Seventy-five Years in California*, pp. viii, 1, 16, 75.)

Capt'n Paty must be doing well at the leward, otherwise he would not have remained so long. I presume he has seen Mr McKinley as I learn that he arrived at San Pedro some time since.

Mr Green the Collector of this Port tells me that should Capt P. bring a cargo to this place from Mexico the laws of the United States would oblige him to exact duties on it notwithstanding the contract he has with General Castro but under the peculiar circumstances of the case he is undecided as yet how to act. Captain Paty may have apprehended some difficulty in this way and has remained below partly for the object of disposing of his cargo, as there has not been any collector appointed yet for the leward ports by the American authority

Mr Beldin at San Francisco was instructed by Captain Paty when he left to dispose of his goods only for immediate pay or to trust those persons whom he felt sure would pay this season but as circumstances have so materially changed during the absence of the "Don Quixote" I have considered it more for the interest of the firm to hurry the goods off our hands as soon as possible while they maintain thier high prices, for goods must fall in price in a very short time.   therefore I have advised Mr Beldin to trust out the balance of goods he may have remaining on hand if possible to those persons who hold Ranches and take notes and as it appears we shall soon have a well organized Government established here and the notes will undoubtedly be good, for should the Rancharos not be able to meet the notes as they become due they will be obliged to sacrafice thier lands for payment.

War being declared with Mexico by the President of the United States, we have every reason to beleive that (even in the event of peace) this territory will ever be held possession of by the Americans. it will prove well for the traders as they all intend next season to push their interest ahead and frighten these rancharos into paying their debts.

The state of the country is now getting more quiet. it is reported that General Castro is on his way to Mexico by land, and that most of his soldiers have left him and returned to their respective homes.

I have enclosed you the two last and *first* "Californians"[11] which will give you a better idea of affairs

---

[11] The first California newspaper was printed on an old Ramage press that was brought to Monterey on the ship *Lagoda*. It was consigned to Don Augustín Zamorano, secretary to Governor Echeandía, and arrived in Monterey in 1834 to be used for printing religious tracts and proclamations.

The press was discovered stored in a room at the government building and was resurrected by Walter Colton who, in partnership with Robert Semple, printed the *Californian,* a one sheet weekly which first appeared in 1846. This first publication had been preceded by three single-sheet announcements of important events.

Benjamin P. Kooser who operated the press, wrote the following description, "The press was an old style Ramage, with stone bed sunk in a wooden frame; the platen was wood – mahogany or Spanish cedar; the railroad was strap iron, well greased and the leverage power was a single thread screw, about the size of a Yankee cider press, of the tub pattern, and of iron. When the lever was drawn forward, it took considerable force to push it back."

Walter Colton wrote of his partner, "He created the materials of our office out of the chaos of a small concern which had been used by a Roman Catholic monk in printing a few sectarian tracts. The press was old enough to be preserved as a curiosity; the mice had burrowed in the balls; there were no rules, no leads, and the type was rusty and all in pi. It was only by scouring that the letters could be made to show their faces. A sheet or two of tin was procured and, with a jack-knife, cut into rules and leads. Luckily we found with the press, the greater part of a keg of ink; and now came the main scratch for paper. None could be found, except what is used to envelop the tobacco of the cigar smoked here by the natives. A coaster had a small supply of this aboard, which we procured."

The first issue of the *Californian* contained news of the declaration of war with Mexico and produced quite an excitement. Copies could not be turned out fast enough to satisfy the demand. Crowds stood waiting, ready to snatch them from the press. The subscription price was moderate, $5. per annum and single copies at 12½¢. The type used was brought to California for printing

than I can write. I also enclose you Commander Stockton's Proclamation.

We have sold on the Invoice brought from the Islands about $13.000 worth, part of it pay down in cash and hides and the balance sure pay this season.

A few days since I received your letter pr "Brooklyn" of June 20. to Capt Paty in which you say that you wrote a few days previous by the "Keoni Ana" which vessel has not yet arrived   some accident must have happened to her. You speak of coming on the Coast a good opportunity will be offered to you by the "Euphemia" as she will arrive on the Coast about the time the Quixote will leave for the Islands.

---

in the Spanish language and as there is no "w" in that language, two "vv"s had to be used wherever a "w" occurred.

The *Lagoda,* which brought this first press to California, was built in 1826 at Canton, Massachusetts. It was intended to name her Ladoga for a Russian lake but the wood carver who made her nameboard for the transom misspelled it and the error was never corrected. After one voyage to California she was sold to Jonathan Bourne of New Bedford and made a fortune for him in her 45 years as a whaler. She was changed from ship rig to bark in 1860 and after a long and useful career, served as a coal barge for the Canadian Pacific Company. Finally the 73-year-old boat was sold to the Japanese for breaking up.

A daughter, as a memorial to her father, created the Bourne Memorial Museum of the Old Dartmouth Historical Society in New Bedford, which houses a half size model of the *Lagoda* fully rigged as a whaler.

The *Californian* was later moved to the more up-and-coming town of San Francisco where it fell into competition with the *California Star* published by Sam Brannan, a Mormon who had arrived on the ship *Brooklyn,* July 31, 1846. Edward Kemble, a printer by trade, and a number of Brannan's Mormon colonists who worked on the publication purchased the *Star* from Brannan, and the *Californian,* and brought out a new publication under the masthead of the *Star and Californian.* This name was shortly changed to *Alta California,* edited by Kemble. From its yellowing pages is found the greatest source of information of the Gold Rush period.

As better equipment arrived from the East, the old Ramage press went a-pioneering to Sonoma, Sutter's Fort, Stockton and Columbia, where it met its doom. It was sold at a sheriff's auction sale and left on the sidewalk to be shipped in the morning. During the night some miscreants dragged it to the middle of the street and burned it for some unknown reason or just for vandalism.

I send by the "Euphemia" my watch to be repaired by Mr Boardman will you oblige me by taking charge of it. I beleive that the only fault with it is that a pin is out of some of the wheels, for when placed on its back it keeps time, and immediatily on turning it on its face something can be heard to fall inside and it immediately stops.

I can think of nothing further to add at present. the Brig sails early tomorrow morning. I am in hopes that something yet may detain the Brig untill the Quixote arrives.

Please remember me to Cousin M, and the children.
Your Affectionate Nephew
Ja's H. Gleason

Letters from California
September 1846 to November 1849

                        Yerba Buena   Sep 14, 1846
To Capt Richardson, Ship Brooklyn, Bodega
dear Sir

  Mrs John Paty is anxious to obtain a passage to Oahu and [I] learn of no earlier opportunity than will be offered by your vessel   the lady has on[e] child and perhaps would like to take a servant with her on the passage. If you could make it convenient to take them please inform me by the earliest opportunity and also the lowest price of the passage and what time you will be likely to leave the coast.

                I am   Your Obedient Servant
                                  Ja's H. Gleason
                                     for John Paty
P. S. Please inform me if you will be likely to touch at Monterey or any other part of the coast previous to your departure for the Sandwich Islands
                                         J. H. G.

[pr "Brooklyn"   Yerba Buena   Sep 17, 1846
To William Paty Esq., Honolulu]
dear Uncle

  The "Brooklyn" is now loading at "Bodega" with lumber to go to the Islands and will touch at Monterey previous to her departure. A person is now about to start for Monterey by land who will take this to be forwarded by her

We arrived at this port on Sunday last the 14th from Monterey & S'ta Cruz 7 days passage. At the latter port we remained 5 days and took on board 15M feet lumber mostly rafters 3 x 4 and 3 x 6 and 20 000 shingles and also the logs for Dr Wood.

The Quixote brought up from the leward 55 Bbls Aguardiente for sale on commission, at Monterey we were not allowed to land a gallon and knowing it would be admitted at Santa Cruz Capt Paty touched at that port on his way up the coast, but before we arrived Governor Mervine despached a courier by land with orders not to allow any liquor to be landed fearing that it might be transported to Monterey by land   on the arrival of the Bark at this port we found that we could land the Aguardiente and immediately obtained a permit from the Alcalde and landed the whole at once and we are now daily expecting orders from Monterey prohibiting the importation of it but fortunately we are to the windward of them once.

Collections in this bay have been very poor this season and there appears very little prospect of collecting much untill next year   it is generally supposed that next season there will be many debts paid as the rancheros begin to feel sensible that if they do not make exertions to settle thier accounts they must l[ose] thier lands, they already find [   ] the existing laws are too severe [on] them. Capt Paty has laid attac[hments] on the property of several pers[ons at] Monterey.

Capt Paty finding no busin[ess] to be done here of any conseque[nce] at present has concluded to sa[il] for the leward as soon as he can possibly get ready. he is very anxious to see McKinley and co[me] to some arrangement with him   this is of more importance

Monterey January 28. 1847

To
Miss Frances A. Gleason
    Plymouth

Dear Sister
        The U.S. Ship "Dale" sails in a few
hours for Panama. Consequently the short

---

come there is good society here now far *better*
than in Plymouth and my beautiful little
Spanish wife (that is to be) Catarina will
make you happy, John, & Herbert, remember
me to them very affectionately and also my
kind grandmother, Sylvia Aunt Cooper, Caroline
and Edward. In haste
    Dearly Your Brother, James,

Miss Frances A. Gleason
    Plymouth
        Mass
        U.S.A.

p U.S. Ship "Dale"

NEW-YORK SHIP APR 22 7 cts

PORTIONS OF JAMES GLEASON'S LETTER TO HIS SISTER, OF JANUARY 28, 1847,
WITH ITS ADDRESSED SELF COVER AND WAX SEAL

KNOW ALL MEN BY THESE PRESENTS, That we, SAMUEL BRANNAN, and Ann L. his wife, of San Francisco, Upper California, for and in consideration of the sum of *One Hundred* Dollars, well and truly paid, the receipt whereof is hereby acknowledged, have this day bargained, sold, released, and do hereby convey unto *James Gleason of San Francisco* all our right, title, and interest, to a certain tract, or parcel of land, in the CITY OF STANISLAUS, and known on the Map of said City as Lot Number (*5*) *Five* in Square Number (*14*) *Fourteen* situated on *Gold* Street *corner of Third street*

TO HAVE, AND TO HOLD The aforesaid granted and bargained premises, with all the rights and privileges thereunto belonging unto *him* the said *James Gleason his* heirs, and assigns *forever*; and we, the said Samuel Brannan, and Ann L. his wife, for ourselves, our heirs, executors, administrators and assigns, do by these presents WARRANT and DEFEND the said *James Gleason his* heirs and assigns, in the title to the aforesaid parcel or plat of land, as above described, from ourselves, our heirs, and assigns *forever* to *his and* their use, and behoof forever. In witness whereof, we William Stout, as Attorney for Samuel Brannan, and Ann L. his wife, hereunto set our hands, and affix our seals, at San Francisco this *Fourteenth* day of *May* in the Year of Our Lord One Thousand Eight Hundred and Forty *nine*

Wm Stout L. S.
Atty. SAMUEL BRANNAN.

Signed, sealed, and delivered
In presence of
D W C Thompson
Alfred Smith

Ann L. Brannan L. S.

A Deed to James Gleason from Sam Brannan and his Wife
Dated May 14, 1849, for a price of $100.00 transferred a lot in the city of Stanislaus.

at pre[s]ent to remaining here where the[re] is but little doing. the Bark will b[e] ready to leave in about three weeks as soon as the few debts are collected that were contracted by Mr Beldin.

It is impossible to say what time the Quixote will be at the Islands I presume within two or three months It is Capt Paty's intention to touch in at Santa Cruz on his way down.

    I remain   Your Affectionate Nephew
             Ja's H. Gleason

P. S. Word has reached this place of the capture of S'ta Barbary, San Pedro, and the Pueblo de Los Angeles. Over these the Stars and Stripes are now floating. Commodore Stockton arrived at San Pedro with about 300 seamen and marines from the "Congress" and marched against General Castro who at his approach broke camp and he and his soldiers fled toward Mexico. Stockton then marched into the city and hoisted the American flag.[1]

               J. H. G.

---

[1] After the American flag was raised at Monterey and Yerba Buena, Commodore Stockton, who had succeeded Sloat as commander of the Pacific Squadron, sailed south in the frigate *Congress* and peacefully occupied Santa Barbara on the fourth of August. Leaving Lieutenant Talbot with a garrison of ten soldiers, Stockton sailed to San Diego.

At the time Commodore Sloat stepped ashore at Monterey, Commandante Castro was at Santa Clara trying to raise men to stamp out the Bear Flag rebellion. Afterwards he planned to use his army against Governor Pio Pico who had been firing bombastic ultimatums at him from Los Angeles. Upon hearing that Monterey had fallen into the hands of the Americans, Castro hurried to Los Angeles, made peace with his old-time enemy, Pio Pico, and together they endeavored to raise an army to drive out these new aggressors. Many proclamations were issued by these two patriots but their calls to arms brought out but two hundred poorly armed followers.

Frémont's forces had now increased to 170 men and were mustered into the regular army as the "Battalion of California Volunteers." The now Major Frémont and Captain Gillespie embarked their forces on board the *Cyane* on July 25th. The vessel was commanded by Samuel du Pont who had been transferred from the *Congress* with San Diego as his destination.

Anchored in that memorable spot off Ballast Point, it is recorded in the log book of the *Cyane* that "at 3, (July 29) the launch and *Alligator* under command of Lieut. Rowan arrived and equipped and the marine guard under command of Lt. Maddox left the ship to take possession of the town of San Diego and hoist the American flag."

A march of five miles brought the landing party to Old Town where the proclamation was read and the flag raised without opposition. Don Juan Bandini and Don Santiago Argüello were interested spectators and received the invaders with every mark of kindness.

By taking San Diego it was hoped to prevent the escape of Castro across the border, and early in July the Americans started closing in on Los Angeles. It took two days for Stockton to drag his cannon from San Pedro and he camped on a high mesa outside the pueblo to await Frémont. On the 13th of August the combined forces marched into Los Angeles expecting a fight, for Castro's forces were rumored to number about 1600 men. The truth was that Castro and Pico had fled to Mexico and their army had melted away, consequently no opposition was encountered.

Stockton established headquarters in an adobe building on north Main Street in Los Angeles and wrote a lengthy report on the successful conquest of California which he dispatched to the national capital by Kit Carson.

Frémont set out on the long march back north to Monterey and Stockton returned to San Pedro where he boarded the *Congress* and sailed to the north leaving Captain Gillespie and a garrison of 50 men to keep the peace in the pueblo of Los Angeles.

Confident that the occupation of California was completed, a big celebration was held in Yerba Buena. However they had not reckoned with the young caballeros who had been raised on revolutions. Gillespie proved to be tactless, lacking in diplomacy and unable to keep from showing his contempt for the Californians. A set of stringent rules of conduct, a few arrests and the revolt was on.

Dragging some old cannon up the hill back of the Plaza in Los Angeles, Gillespie's men dug a fort and prepared to defend themselves. They repulsed every attack but it was only a matter of time until their food would run out. A courier named John Brown, but called "Juan Flaco" or "Lean John," rode to the north with the bad news, making the five hundred miles in five days, a remarkable record even in that land of dashing horsemen. When he arrived at Yerba Buena with the news of the revolt, the *Savannah* sailed south with all speed.

Frémont embarked on the *Sterling* but met the *Vandalia* on the way and learned that no horses could be obtained in the southland and so resolved to return to Monterey to secure mounts for his battalion.

Gillespie had capitulated and was allowed to retreat to San Pedro where opportunely Captain Mervine arrived with the *Savannah*. Now with a force of four hundred men, including Gillespie's fifty, a march was planned on Los Angeles. At the Dominguez Rancho they were met by a company of mounted Californians, with one small cannon which, drawn by taut reatas, was wheeled into position, fired, and dragged out of range. This form of attack so demoralized the Americans that they retreated to their ship with their dead and wounded. The six men slain were buried on Dead Man's

Letters from California, 1846-1849

[pr U.S. Ship "Dale"] Monterey January 28, 1847
To Miss Frances A. Gleason, Plymouth
Dear Sister

The U.S. ship "Dale"[2] sails in a few hours for Panama consequently the short time allowed me to improve the opportunity to write compells me to be as brief as possible. The Bark "Don Quixote" is now absent to the Islands. She has been absent two months. I am now expecting her daily with a cargo of provisions. The U.S. forces now on this coast are short of supplies   Consequently there is every probability of Uncle John selling his *whole cargo* for *cash* on his arrival   he will undoubtedly make by the voyage clear of all expences (allowing him to obtain a suitable cargo at Oahu) from 14,000.$ to 20,000.$, I mention this for my grandmother's information.

I am now acting as General Agent for Paty & Co. on this coast and have now in my charge an Invoice of goods amounting to $20,000; landed from the Don

---

Island which stood at the entrance to the harbor. The bodies were later removed to the Military Cemetery at San Francisco when Dead Man's Island was dredged out in order to widen the main channel of San Pedro Harbor.

The whole southland was now in rebellion and San Diego was retaken. After some heavy cannonading and real battles, the Californians gave up the struggle and this war was over.

[2] The 16-gun ship-sloop *Dale,* built in 1839, measured 117'-7" between perpendiculars, 33'-10" moulded beam and 15'-0" depth in the hold. She was armed with 16 carronades, 32 pounders, and was a handy ship with a fair turn of speed. (Howard Irving Chapelle, *The History of American Sailing Ships,* N.Y., 1949.) With the Pacific Squadron in 1841, under the leadership of Captain ap Catesby Jones, she partook of the active and complicated maneuvers of training, and nearly equalled the frigate *United States* on most points of sailing. When Captain Jones set out for his ill-advised expedition to Monterey from Callao, the *Dale* was ordered to Panama with dispatches for Washington.

In December of 1848, the Pacific Squadron lay in San Francisco Bay, with Captain Jones complaining that the crews were deserting for the mines.

Quixote when she left for the Islands. I have been very uneasy since I have had this amount of property in my possession, as an attack has been daily expected upon this town for the last two months by the Californian forces   all the streets have been baracaded and residents obliged for thier safety to pass through the streets armed. I write this with a brace of pistols at my side — I have had several escapes from being taken prisioner — I have not time to give you particulars — suffice it to say that I am yet safe. We do not fear much danger now however as the arrival of the U.S. Ship "Independence" a few days since gives us more security.

My last letter to you was by the "Levant" since then I have purchased three house lots in San Francisco which will in a few years hence be valued at $8000, or $10,000.   they are all excellent lots   one of them is on the front of "Portsmouth Square" in the centre of the (what will soon be) *Metropolis*   I shall commence building as soon as my means will allow me so to do. I have a lot also in this town which will soon be vary valuable. It is astonishing to see how fast emigrants are coming to this country both by sea and land since it has been added to the United States. I have been on this coast now ten months and have acquired a knowledge of the Spanish language and become acquainted with the people and country consequently my chance of *making a fortune* is somewhat more promising than that of thousands now arriving strangers in the country. A young man arrived here in the "Independence" a few days since by the name of Atherton   his brother is wealthy and has a very influential house in Valparaiso   he wishes to make an arrangement with me to establish a Commission House in Yerba Buena. I shall however await the arrival of the Don Quixote before I make any new arrangements.

There is but one thing in this world dear sister that makes me unhappy   it is the thought of your unpleasant circumstances at home.   it is a long time since I have received news from you   affairs may have materially changed with you, you may be married, and happy. I ardently hope so, write to me by the earliest opp'y and say if you wish to come to California if you do I will have no expence spared to have you come   there is good society here now *far better than in Plymouth* and my beautiful little Spanish wife (that is to be) Catarina will make you happy. John, & Herbert, remember me to them very affectionately and also my kind grandmother, Sylvia Aunt Cooper, Caroline and Edward. In haste
 Dearly Your Brother,   James
You can direct letters to me as follows Monterey California care of Talbot H. Green[3] Merchant by vessels coming direct or by the way of the Hawaiian Islands.
 James

[pr U.S. Ship "Prebble"
To Miss Frances A. Gleason, Plymouth]
 Monterey California   May 2, 1847
My dear Sister

I have just finished my fourth business letter to the Sand'ch Islands — lit my cigar — and now I am ready to devote my time to a dear acquaintance. I am not married yet but tomorrow I intend to ask for the hand of Catarina Watson, *we must be united,* she is one of

---

[3] Talbot H. Green, a prominent merchant of San Francisco, was nominated for Mayor in 1850 but while walking down Montgomery Street, was recognized by a man who had known him in the east as a Paul Geddes who had disappeared under peculiar circumstances. This discovery created a great scandal but Talbot stoutly denied the rumors and offered to go east and clear his name and reputation. He did not return to California in time for the election nor for several years after!

the loveliest — sister that the world can boast of — a disposition that an angel might envy, her father is a merchant in this place, worth about 30,000,$ and I have a rival sole heir to about 50,000,$ these are large numbers however I have hopes of success   Kate tells me that she loves me — that she will wed me and no other — David Spence,[4] my rival, has been her companion from infancy yet my happy disposition and *good looks* has removed from her all the attachments she had to him and the charm of *Fifty thousand*. I am received into the family as a favorite   I have shared at Mr Watsons[5] table for more than five months and he will not receive anything for my board and her mother extends to me a thousand kindnesses that would be refused an older acquaintance.

There is not a young man[6] in California with more promising prospects before him that are now presented to me   Mr Watson is aware of this and this encourages me to hope for success. I am acting at present as Agent for Paty & Co on this Coast. I have a large establishment in this place and the whole cargo of the

---

[4] David E. Spence was born in Scotland and in 1824 came to California from Lima, Peru, aboard the English brig *Pizarro* to superintend the meat packing plant of Gregg and Company at Monterey, going into business for himself in 1827. He married Doña Adelaida, daughter of Don Mariano Estrada.

[5] James Watson was born in London of Scotch parents and was baptized into the Catholic church at Monterey in 1830 as Santiago Pedro Watson, with J. B. Cooper acting as his godfather. He married Mariana Escamilla at the San Carlos Mission the same year and the marriage resulted in twelve children, nine of whom reached maturity. James Henry Gleason married one of the daughters, who was baptized at San Carlos Mission as María Catarina Demetria Watson. James Watson died in 1863 and was buried at the mission of San Antonio. (Amelia Kneass, former curator of the Robert Louis Stevenson Museum, Monterey, California.)

[6] At the time of the writing of this letter, James Henry Gleason was twenty-four years of age, having been eighteen when he first arrived in the Sandwich Islands in 1841.

"Don Quixote" two months since brought from Oahu was placed in my hand for sale. I have not determined as yet whether to join the firm of Paty & Co as a partner or Establish myself in California as a Commission Merchant

You must excuse me for a few moments my servant has just brought into the office a piece of pie. I wish I could share with you   it looks so nice.

         15 minutes later
Having ate my pie — smoked a cigar — walked the terrace, blowed my nose, and censured the servant for a blunder I again return to you. — I am thinking of a subject to commence upon — here's one at once.

The above ten lines I filled with nonsense   I must quit that for I pay 1.50¢ postage for this letter in advance.

Sister I wish you were in California I would immediately find you a *happy home*. Every letter that I receive from you I open with the expectation of reading "I am married" and every line breathing happiness. I would that your days were as happy as mine.   nearly every afternoon a pic-nic in the wods with the Senoritas and nearly every night a dance.   our music the guitar and harp and for a partner a spanish maiden whose very existence is *Love*. I imagine myself associated with Angels while moving around in a waltz with these lovely beings   thier very language — the Castillian — is sufficient to warm the coldest heart when they speak of *Love*.   while writing this my thoughts naturally revert to Kate, I imagine that I see her expressive eyes beaming upon me in the ball-room. Kate — tomorrow decides our fate whether we are to pass our future days happy or miserable. We will now change the subject.

I have lately bought three large lots of land in this town about 300 yards. I intend to build me a house on one of the lots this year   the other two I bought for speculation   I have also two excellent house lots in the town of San Francisco   these lots will be very valuable in a few years hence. California is a new country just springing into existence and it is astonishing to see with what rapidity it is progressing   within four months fifty buildings have been commenced in the town of San Francisco. Should California increase for the next ten years as it has for the last Six months I realize that my land that I now own will be worth at least 15. or 20.000$ for my land is now nearly in the centre of the town   The authorities in this town in order to bring me into notice have named one of the principal streets *Gleason Street* I was not aware of this honor untill I saw a deed of land made out and noticed that one side was bounded by "Gleason Street"!!

The "Don Quixote" left this port the 8th of March last for Oahu and it is uncertain whether she will return to this coast again from the Islands or make a voyage to Valpairaso or China   it will depend entirely upon whether she will be able to obtain a good cargo for this market in Oahu which I think is very doubtful as a number of vessels have lately ar'vd on this Coast from the Islands bringing full cargoes   this would make goods scarce and high at that place

Should the Barque return direct to this coast, she ought to be here at any hour.

It is a long while since I have received a line from you. I shall expect letters from home by the next arrival from the Sandwich Islands. You can write to me always by the way of the Sandwich Islands, or by direct opportunity to California, direct your letters J. H. Gleason,

California, care of Talbot H. Green Monterey and I will be sure to receive them,

Why does not Cousin Caroline write me she has much more time to write than I have Remember me to her very affectionately.

Aunt Mary Ann has presented us with another Cousin born the first day of January last at Oahu, a girl.

Please give my love to all particularly my Grandmother.

Tell John and Herbert that I am anxious to hear from them.

Su mui Afectisimo Hermano
Santiago

[the kindness of F. Teschmaker Esq]
Monterey May 22d 1847
To Miss Frances A. Gleason, Plymouth
My dear Sister

Mr. Teschmaker an intimate friend of mine takes his departure for the U. States. he thinks of visiting Plymouth in his pleasure trips through the United States should you see him extend to him your usual good kindness. I am ashamed to know that he will become acquainted with the condition of Father's intemperate habits as it will make me feel disagreeable whenever I meet him afterwards, however, Sister, prove to him through your good kindness and civility that *our family* is worthy of his acquaintance if our *father* is not. God send that our Father has reformed, should he still be intemperate pursuade him sister to preserve respectability while my friend is in Plymouth as I now associate with the highest class of society in California.

It is but a few days since that I wrote to you across land which letter will probably reach you in less than three months from date giving you a full account of my circumstances   consequently I shall be brief in this as I am very much pressed for time and my friend Tesch will give you my history *in full*.

For Grandmother

Barque "Don Quixote" is sold for $9500, at Oahu — Uncle J. has purchased a schooner for 4500.$ and is expected on the Coast daily with a cargo of $8000. — Paty & Co doing a good business — very apparently. My kind remembrance to my grandmother. —

Well Sister, I am engaged to Kate Watson. Not to be married however for eighteen months at least as she is young only 15 years.

I did not intend to write by this opportunity having written but a few days since and eight months will pass ere this reaches you. I would not have written had it not been that Tesch. informed me at the last moment that if I wished it he would visit Plymouth, consequently he has been waiting for me while I have scratched off the preceding lines   you can judge my hurry by the writing

In brief   My love to all
Your Affectionate Brother
James

[To Miss Frances A. Gleason, Plymouth]

Monterey   30 May 1847
Night   11 O.oclock

My Affectionate Sister

You must excuse me if my letter may be brief as

I have seized my pen at a late hour after passing the day in the confusion of business. Capt Paty will write and will of course inform you in relation to business, therefore I shall merely say that I remain here for several months hence while Capt Paty sails for the leward   I have in my charge for sale part of the cargo that the schooner brought from the Islands.

It is but a few days since that I wrote to you by a very intimate friend Mr Teschmaker who has taken his departure for Boston in the ship "Loo Choo"   to please me he will visit Plymouth while at home   I have given him a letter of introduction to you.   he is of a very wealthy family and it annoys me exceedingly to know that he will become acquainted with my father's intemperate habits. I know that you will prove to him sister through your kindness that he is worthy our acquaintance.   he will give you considerable information about me.

I have *popped the question* for the hand of that lovely girl Catarina Watson   her parents wish me to wait for 18 months and then ask for her again as she is too young to marry only 14 years of age   She tells me that she will have me and none other   we often speak of you in our *love chats*   she wishes you to come to her country, — to her home.   her father is worth about 40,000.$ I am now enjoying the happiest days of my life nothing but Pic-nic's and dances. I only feel unhappy when my thoughts turn towards home and think of you, were you here I could provide you a happy home. I have not the least hopes of your coming were I to send for you, as you are too deeply in love.

I have lately purchased about 400 yards of land in the center of this town   I have about 100 yards also in San Francisco. I intend to build me a house in this place as soon as I get over my hurry. Should California increase in population and business for 5 years as it has lately my house lots will become very valuable. Since California has become an American Territory we have every reason to believe that it will flourish rapidly. This is the country now for an active young man to prosper I consider I have the advantage of hundreds of strangers now emigrating to this coast as I am acquainted with the country the people and the Spanish language. I often think of the happy circumstances that brought me to the Pacific, had I remained at home I would have been *nobody* as it is I have acquired a talent for business mended my boyish rascality and carelessness and found a happy and contented home in a foreign land, with promising prospects of a *fortune* if not in dollars – in *Kate Watson.*

Drowsiness and a bad pen obliges me to quit. good night

In brief — you know who to remember me to. – Grandmother particularly.

Your Affectionate Brother   James

Monterey California Aug 12/47

To Miss Frances A. Gleason, Plymouth

My dear Sister

I must write in haste being exceedingly busy.

Say to Grandmother that I am daily looking for Uncle John he has been absent about two months to the leward. He has sold out nearly all of his cargo and I presume that on his return to this port he will proceed to Oahu to purchase another cargo. My latest dates from the Sandwich Islands is 31st June '47 our friends were all well.

On the return of Uncle John from the leward I expect I shall go to San Francisco to collect the debts of Paty & Co. as there will be no interest to keep me at this place having nearly sold out my stock of merchandise.

I am now building me a store in this place the workmen are now putting on the roof it will cost me when finished about 1500.$ my intention is at present to rent it untill I establish myself in business which will eventually be in this place as I never was more pleased with a spot on earth not even excluding my birthplace — here the society is united which makes our public balls and parties pass in the most harmonious manner, and here has grown my affection for the girl that is to cheer my whole future days as a wife — Kate Watson, could you but see her. She is the pride of Monterey, you do not know Frances how a Spanish girl can love could you but look in upon us while alone and listen to her endearing sentiments and watch the sparkling lustre of her eyes it would make your heart dance with rapture. — Kate takes a tour in the country while I am absent to San Francisco she often speaks of you and wishes to see you.

Sister — notwithstanding the warm attachments and the interest that binds me to this country I still sustain the hope of revisiting Plymouth at some future day, — may Providence give us one more paternal embrace.

Please remember me to all particularly Grandmother.

Your Affectionate Brother *James*

[Fav'r of J. J. Jarves Esq.
To Miss Frances A. Gleason, Plymouth U.S.A.]

                              Pueblo de Los Angeles
                         California   April 1 1848

Dearly Beloved Sister

    Yesterday I received four letters from home forwarded to me from Honolulu which came to the Pacific in the Schooner "Honolulu" viz John's of date Sept 23d 1847, Herbert's of Feb. 17, 1847, Wm. B. Gleason & Sam'l Gleason of Feb 16 1847. For these letters I beg you will extend my warmest thanks to my Brothers & Cousins for their kind remembrance of me and say that the "Barnstable" sails from this Coast on the 1st of next month direct for the United States and by her I will answer these kind letters now before me, which they have been pleased to send me. I cannot understand why you have not written by this opp'y, if you knew sister how I value your letters, how often I read them over, and the pleasure and joy they give me when recieving them you would not neglect me   California is now my home, and the longer I remain in this land the more I become attached to it and through a vista of long years I cannot point out a period when I can return to you. I learn from Wm B. Gleason's Letter that you are really to be married to your Agustus.   well I hope some day to recieve you both at my home in California. I am also engaged to a wealthy and beautiful Spanish Lady   it is three weeks since I left Monterey where our tears mingled at parting and her last dulces palabras "pronto vuelve, amardo Santiago mio" yet dwells upon my ears with all the sweetness of a — sugar kiss. however we will meet again in four weeks Catalina mia and ——— dance the wild Polka once more.   for the last two years there has nothing been thought of by the Californians but diversion and it has been one continual round of pleasure and joy, it has appeared to me like a dream. I am a particular favourite with the Californians and there is not a house on the Coast but what I am recieved into with all the freedom of one of the family.   a Ball or Mereanda cannot pass off alegre without the presence of Santiago. Doña Nacisa de Osio is now waiting my return to Monterey to give me a splendid Ball. I have often wished you could see me at times traveling up and down the coast in my California riding dress, sometimes camping out in the mountains surrounded by wild indians and bears other times at some rancho luxuriating on a bullock hide stretched out over a few sticks, at other times dressed up in fine broad cloth at the house of a rich family as I am at present while writing this with Doña Arcadia & Isadora pursuading me every few moments to lend them my voice while the latter is running her delicate fingers over the harp strings. I tell them that I am writing to Francisca my sister and they tell me to mention their "expresiones y saludes" to you.

I have a good prospect for the future and I am in hopes in a number of years to acquire a fortune   I have a house building in Monterey which ought to be finished now   it will cost 1600$ or 1800$ I have besid[es] this in Monterey about 350 yards [of] land in house lots. I own also in San Francisco a house lot of 50 yards which I have leased and I own in Benecia 3 more house lots   I can call all this my own property and clear from debt and I value it worth 5000$. this day. I purchased this land very cheap before the Am. flag was hoisted in California   the land I have in S. Fran'co cost me 200.$ and I have been offered for it 1400.$

I am now at this place settling up the old accounts of Paty & Co. I am expecting the Malek Adhel[7] daily from San Diego. Uncle John is on board master and owned jointly by Paty & Co and Wm. D. Phelps. I have just [com]pleted a trip up and down the Coast in the Malek Adhel collecting Accounts and with an Invoice of goods making sales. Uncle John remained during the time at San Francisco in the Sch'r Mary Ann which was chartered at the islands by Paty & Co.   he has now finished the voyage and sent her back to Honolulu and joined me in the "Malek Adhel". The M. Adhel was bought by Paty & Co & Phelps 5 months since at Monterey for 4500.$ she was captured by the U.S. Ship "Cyane" at Mazatlan from the Mexicans and brought to California and sold by order of the Court of Admiralty at Monterey. it is the same vessel that caused so much excitement in the U. States about the time I left home. She was taken at sea on suspisious [of] being a slaver and was taken to New York condemned and sold.   at that time I little expected now to be supercargo of her and have for a Captain the same person that commanded the Brig Regulator when she was lost on Browns island in Plymouth a few years before I left home — Captain Phelps says it was the hardest time of his life   As soon as the Brig arrives we intend to leave immediately for the Northward ports   Uncle John will go to the islands in six or

---

[7] The U.S. *Warren* anchored off Mazatlan and found the Mexican brig *Malek Adhel* lying near the mole in the process of being stripped of her sails preparatory to being towed up the creek for safety. Captain Hull sent a launch with sixty men to cut the vessel out, whereupon the Mexicans, deserting the ship, fled without firing a shot. The *Warren* supplied a set of sails and the *Malek Adhel* arrived in Monterey in October of 1846, with a prize crew, to report her own capture. She was sold to Captains William Phelps and John Paty for $4900.00 and traded on the coast with Captain Phelps as master and James Henry Gleason as supercargo.

Eight months to live and place his business with me to settle up on the Coast. I expect soon to be permanently established in business in Monterey.

My next letter will be by the "Barnstable" Remember me very affectionately to Grandmother Sylvia Aunt Cooper Caroline & Edward John & Herbert, your Augustus &c.
       Your very Affectionate Brother
            James

[pr "Barnstable"]   Pueblo de Los Angeles
            May 18 1848
To Miss Frances A. Gleason, Plymouth
My dear Sister

How very disappointed I am in not receiving letters from home by this vessel. the "Olga" just arrived having a short passage of 129 days from Boston. not one line, yet I can blame no one for I could not for one moment beleive that you being aware of an opportunity to write me would let it pass unnoticed, and also dear sister I have to mention that a few weeks since I received letters from John Herbert William & Sammell Gleason by way of Honolulu I believe that you must have written and the letter is by some accident mislaid.

I hardly know how to write a letter now in english, this learning kanaka and spanish has played the duece with what little *I did* know of the english language. if you would ask for a letter in spanish I would give you a dozen in half an hour and decent, respectable ones at that. You had quite a compliment paid to you last evening a lovely young Donña while I was waltzing with her whispered "Have you a sister Don Santiago?" yes I replied but far from here. "then you must send for her" she said "for a sister of yours must be una hermosura perfecto" I thanked her for our joint compliment that she paid us. By the way I engaged to ride out with her this afternoon and it is time that I was preparing. this circercumstance now has reminded me of it — I must leave you for a while.

Sunday eve — Instead of going to the theatre I am penning this, by the light of two miserable tallow candles one placed in a bottle and the other in a saucer erected by its own elements this is a circumstance which you must attribute not to my poverty but to my neglect in observing that the lamps were not trimmed before night and now my servant is off perhaps on some drunken spree or at the gambling table to waste his weeks wages in what he may call pleasure. My stars how it thunders in the mountains. it seems as though the Heavens and Earth were in deadly conflict at the same time the full clear moon is throughing (That last word was spelled beautifully) her beams through my window slap upon my back. the music at the theatre which is close by rings upon my soul or ears. I would say and the united power and influence of the three — Thunder, Moon, & Music, has as you will readily perceive by my scribbling filled my ideas with a combination of poetry & nonsence.

I would like very much to sit me down if it could be but once only, and write a proper and sensible letter to you and my friends at home. I have the ideas in my head but somehow they will not come out when they are most required. If I were to read my letters over after writing them you might be certain never to receive one from me, for I invariably tear them up after perusing them. I cannot trust myself to the reading of them they appear to me so confounded foolish and of course they are and must be thus apparent to you.

Letters from California, 1846-1849

I would have you believe that your most affectionate brother Santiago has some sense and regularity about him but I must confess that you cannot give me credit for a shadow of either even were you so disposed judging from my epistles home, however I pray you will be lenient and consider that I have passed the last six years "de me vida" among arabs and fed myself on *California Beans & Bullocks greese* thanks to Providence I got fat upon it though and have a fair prospect of seeing this world's vanity for 80 or 100 years yet without some horse kicks me, or shot in a duel. The candle is growing dim and I have no snuffers, however I'll take my fingers. Juanito Bandini[8] my friend here on the left is snoaring gaily, laying half uncovered – beautiful being of nature – sleep on, (next sheet) I will try to change my ideas with a new sheet [of the letter].

I am now preparing for a journey for San Francisco a distance of 600 miles   I have purchased six horses and want three more for my boy "Friday"   these I am in hopes to obtain tomorrow and about Wednesday heigh ho! for the north — to my Catalina — the star of my pathway through life — the beacon that guides me to happiness. Twelve days will bring me to thy arms. — to once more forget the world in thy presence — to gaze (candle in the saucer has just fallen) in those large melting expressive eyes and "ser feliz contigo." Yesterday I received a letter from Monterey informing me that my store is nearly finished and is a very pretty building   I expect it will cost me nearly $1800. Mr

---
[8] Juan Bandini, a native of Peru, married Dolores Estudillo and owned several large ranchos in the southwest. When Commodore Robert Stockton was in San Diego the Bandinis entertained him and his officers with dancing parties and music at both of which Juan was very adept. (Hubert H. Bancroft, *History of Celifornia,* 7 vols., San Francisco, 1884-90.)

Eli Southworth [9] and myself own it jointly, our intention is to rent it untill I have arranged Paty & Co's business so as to establish myself on shore   I am now travelling up and down the coast recovering debts and speculating   Paty & Co. have sold thier interest in the Brig "Malek Adhel" owing to her not being a proper vessel for the California trade   she carried but very little cargo. Uncle John will purchase the first vessel that he meets with if she pleases him and offered for sale. I have no doubt but what he will soon have a chance to buy one when he arrives above.   he is writing to Grandmother and I presume he will give her particulars with regard to business &c so I will drop it merely mentioning that we are getting along finely. I received letters from the islands a few weeks since — all well and gay. Uncle William writes me that Mr Gordon of Plymouth has interested himself nobly in the cause of the Paty family   he is overjoyed with this unlooked for act of kindness. I do not well remember Mr Gordon   I beg you will write me about him. he has a generous and noble heart and his disinterested kindness to our Grandmother will ever claim a place in my memory

          Noche 23d

For the last few days I have been confined in court as juror on the trial of 3 Mormon Officers for passing counterfeit coin and now I catch at a moment to close this while the boy is preparing the horses for our journey. I wrote to you a few weeks since by the way of

---

[9] Eli Southworth came out to California from Boston aboard the *Loriot* on the longest trip on record, two hundred days. He was a clerk for William Heath Davis, at whose home he died in 1857. (Davis, *Seventy-five Years in California*, p. 253.)

Mexico, a double letter and hope that it will have come to hand ere you receive this.

Wishing you every happiness   My very dear sister
            I remain   Your Affec't Brother
                                           James

This finishes my 10th letter

[Kindness of Mr Chnshir
pr U.S. Ship "Warren"]
                        Monterey   California   July 20 1848
To Miss Frances A. Gleason, Plymouth, Mass
My very dear sister

I will give you a few lines which will show you that I have not quite forgotten you although I have but a few moments to write. I have just returned from an evening's visit to my Catharine and her playful smiles yet dwell on my imagination and play the duece with my ideas.

A very rich gold mine has lately been discovered about 250 miles north of this place and everybody in the country is rapidly hastening towards it[10]   about

---

[10] After the occupation of California by the Americans, the rancheros settled down to the raising of cattle, hides still being the medium of exchange in a moneyless land. It was a contented existence, with Indian vaqueros to do the work and the hacienda the center of social activities where every event was celebrated with a fandango. A romantic pastoral life had been created which was soon to be rudely disturbed, for in January 1848, a Mormon in the employ of John Sutter, noted in his diary, "Monday 24th: This day some kind of mettle was found in the tailrace that looks like goald first discovered by James Martial the Boss of the Mill."

Marshall hastened to notify his boss, John Sutter, of the discovery and was admonished to secrecy, for if the news got out, Sutter's plans for the principality of New Helvetia (Sacramento) would be ruined by a stampede of gold-mad people. The news however was too good to keep and before long an influx of Mormons appeared at the mill and frantically searched the river bottom for nuggets. Soon gold began to appear in San Francisco and the secret

1,000,000.$ has already been extracted from the mine persons of my acquaintance who could only show 2 months since 100.$ can now count their 10,000 or 15000.$ Many have obtained daily with trifling expense $800. others 600. & 400. &c about 4000 persons are now at the mines and no one that works obtains less than 1 oz of gold pr day this is the least. I myself have seen about $100000. in different persons hands, every body is getting wealthy. the mines cover in extent of about 300 square miles and gold sufficient for 5000 men to work for 20 years. Such a discovery has never been known since the commencement of the world. it appears to us as a dream — too much for reality. all kinds of merchandise command high prices, Shovels and pick axes which the gold diggers require are sold at 16 to 20.$ each. Flour 40.$ Barrel a common blanket I have seen sold for 60.$ ordinary clerks receive 200.$ salary pr *month* I have been offered 250.$ pr month to take goods to the mines for sale cooks & servants get 50.$ month. the excitement is tremendous. We anticipate great trouble in the country in a few months as the farmers are leaving their crops to go to the "Placer" or gold mine and we beleive that provisions will not be brought into the country to supply the demand. we must depend upon importations for our existance as nothing will be

---

was out. It is surprising how quickly the news spread in those days before the telegraph. Ships all over the world altered their courses to this El Dorado by the Western Sea and the Gold Rush was on.

Since the overland trip was impossible in midwinter, the first contingents came by the fever-infested Isthmus of Panama, while the New Englanders with their tradition of sea and sail, chose the all-water route around Cape Horn where the seasons are reversed.

Before the discovery of gold San Francisco numbered about fifty one-story buildings, with a population of 375. During 1849 nearly 40,000 people landed there on the way to the diggings and 549 vessels of all descriptions had passed through the Golden Gate.

raised in the country. the crews of vessels desert immediately on arrival. two vessels were on the point of making a voyage to the Co'l River for Flour and when all was prepaired not a person was to be found on board.

I am anxiously awaiting the arrival of Uncle John from the leward coast I expect him daily. I only arrived here a few days since from the Pueblo by land where I left Uncle John about embarking and (tell my grandmother) in good health. On his arrival we will immediately make preparations to go to the mines, where we expect in a few years to make our independent fortunes and return amongst you to pass the remainder of our lives.

I have not exagerated in the least in my account of the gold mines you can place the utmost confidence in the story. The Govenor has just returned to this place from a visit to the mine and I have given you here his account which agrees with hundreds of others. he also says that 5000 men in 300 days with cheap machines can obtain gold sufficient to pay the expenses of the war w[it]h Mexico,

$$\begin{array}{r} 5000 \text{ men} \\ \underline{30.\$ \text{ daily}} \\ 150.000 \\ \underline{300 \text{ days}} \\ 45.000.000 \end{array}$$

All improvements in townships which has been so rapidly advancing is now suddenly stopped and 20 men cannot be found in this place and less in San Francisco.

I have lately received letters from Oahu all our friends are well. Uncle William tells me that 5 vessels have lately arrived there from the U. States and not one line was received from home. I tell you Fanny you must

write   you must not be so neglectful   it seems an age since I have heard from you   are you married and so deeply interested in your ——————— that you have forgotten us. Love to all. — In haste
    Your Affectionate Brother James

        San Blas   Feb. 28, 1849
To Miss Frances A. Gleason, Plymouth

 For the last few days I have been confined to my couch with the chills & fever. I am now gaining my health and am able to rise proped up by pillows to send you a few lines merely to acquaint you of my whereabouts.

 I have come to Mexico to purchase a cargo for California on joint A/c with Cap't Paty   each advances $10,000 & a good prospect of making good sales.

 We sail for Mazatlan in 10 or 12 days from which place I will write you a long letter.

 Why have I not rec'd a line from you for nearly a year? it is unacountable.

 I am now in a fair way to make a fortune in a few years. I value my property now in Calf'a worth $15,000 & owe no debts.

 I am anxious to have you all in Calif'a and I shall endeavour to have you come.

 Even writing these few lines has fatigued me exceedingly. Good night, Your Affec't Brother
           James

    Bark Mary Frances   March 17/49
To Miss Frances A. Gleason, Plymouth
Dear beloved Sister

 Our sails are loosed to take us to California. I have

been unwell for 8 or 10 days but am now rapidly recovering. I have come to Mexico on a speculating voyage. Capt Paty & myself have on board $20,000. worth of goods on joint account. I think we will do well with it in California.

Mr Ja's Doten has just arrived here direct from Plymouth & takes passage with us for California   he tells me that he was introduced to you at a party on Billington Sea.   he says that I ought to be proud of such a "beautiful girl" for a sister   I got no letters by him as he did not expect to see me   It is a long while since I have received a letter from you. As the steamers now offer a speedy conveyance I must have you write often. You have probably ere this heard of the discovery of the gold mines in Calif'a   Through its happy influence I am rapidly acquiring a fortune, last summer I was on the mines 10 days and made 1800.$ had I not got sick I could have made 8 or 10.000.$ I wish my brothers were there   they could make more in 24 hours than they could in 1 year at home. I now value myself worth with my land and gold 15.000.$

Love to all
Your Affectionate Brother — James

[Postmark: New York Ship, May 25, 7 cts]

San Francisco   June 20 1849

To Miss Frances A. Gleason, Plymouth
My dear Sister

I am now about embarking on board the "Panama" for Monterey where I intend to establish myself in business. Coz M, and her family are with me   they continue on to the U.S. and you obtain from her considerable information respecting my affairs which I have not time to write about being exceedingly busy. I send by her three pounds of gold for pocket and pin money and a small lot that I washed out of the earth myself last summer   this last lot you must have made into jewelry   you will prize this much as I nearly forfeited my life in washing for it for 3 days   I was on the edge of the grave   I shall never visit the mines again   I can coin money fast enough in this country by speculating. I shall send you more gold when less pressed for payments   I have to pay in a few days about $7000. and have not more than enough to meet the Bills. You must write to me by *every steamer*, direct you letters to me at Monterey care of James Watson Tell John & Herbert that I give them a house lot each in Monterey   I have not time to write them. I think of visiting P. in a few months and will bring them out with me.

Love to all   Your Affec't Brother
James

Monterey Nov'r 15/49

Doña Francesca Gleason, Plymouth
My dear Sister

Well Fanny I'm married. My bonny Kate is now reclining over my shoulder & anxious to know what I am about to say, to my sister.   she understands but few words in english. She saw "My" & "Kate" in the second line and knew what it meant at once but the "bonny" which intervenied was a damper. I told her it was saltfish and she curled her pretty lip and tapped me under the chin with all the gentleness of a boy eating a peice of pumpkin pie.

I was married on the 7th of Oct at 3 Oc in the morning. a large dinner party was given by my father at his house in the afternoon and a dance followed in the evening. the expenses must have been nearly $1000. I am living in Monterey & have Uncle John's family remaining with me at present on a visit I have established myself here in business a general wholesale and retail under the head of Gleason & Co. my partner is a german. To give you an idea of our speculations I will mention that yesterday I bought 200 Bbls Flour @ 20.$ pr Barrel and today advices from San Francisco quote flour at 50.$ I am about shipping it now to that port where I am in hopes to clear between 4 & 5000.$ I was offered 30.$ a barrel for it this afternoon & refused it. I shall leave tomorrow in the steamer for San Francisco having purchased an invoice of china goods to the am't of 10,000.$ I am obliged to go & attend to the sale of it.

I was exceedingly pleased to receive letters from home by the last steamer. My relatives & friends must pardon me if I do not answer their letters promptly people value their time here at the rate of $10. a minute. letters from John, Herbert, Edward, Caroline, Sylvia, Wm. B. Gleason, Father, A. Tribble Geo. White I. T. Hall & yourself have come safely to hand & I beg you say to each one that I give them my heartiest thanks for their remembrance of me.

I cannot advise my brothers to come to this country at present. I have reflected well upon this & had I deemed it advantageous to them I would have had them here this day, but I came to the conclusion that they were better at home it is only the smartest kind of men that can push their way through here and also it requires capital a person cannot lay idly when his personal expenses are from 8 to 12.$ pr day & interest

10% pr month.   there are thousands now in the country seeking employment & suffering for the want of funds to support themselves with   If my brothers choose to shoulder thier pick & spade & risk their lives in the mines slaveing themselves from morn till night for their ounce of gold they can come   it is the only chance now open.   it is different from last year let my brothers be assured that I am for thier interest and whenever I can feel myself safe in recommending thier journeying this way I will not fail to call them. I may be worth 30,000.$ to day & tomorrow a poor man, my knowledge of the country gives me great advantage.

 I have much to say but must delay untill the next steamer.   you must not fail to write by every mail & I will endeavour to do the same   My wife joins me in love to you all.

Your Affec't Brother James

4

Letters from San Francisco and Monterey, December 1849 to 1859

                        San Francisco   Dec'r 31. 1849
To Herbert Gleason Esq.
My dear Brother
   I have the pleasure to acknowledge the receipt of a number of voluminous letters of a late date from your hands and am pleased to notice by glancing them through how much you have improved in your composition within the last few years. I can hardly realize that the letters before me were written by the little bread & molasses boy that used to hang about my legs while I was at home.
   Well Herbert we have not been so badly educated after all.   you have been thrown into the office of Secretary and as for me they wanted to raise me to Judge of Monterey Court & finding that I would not accept of it they wanted me to run for one of the assembly as alderman but I would not listen to it and now they want to shove me in Collector for Monterey. confound them they humbug my very soul out. I have so much business on my hands that I want nothing to do with Public offices. I have been absent from Monterey six weeks during which time I have made 2000.$ clear in a little Flour speculation and bought ¼ of a cargo of 100,000 ft lumber at the rate of $360. pr thousand ft for the Sacramento City market   my last advises from that place quote lumber at a fraction less

than $500.m   the cargo was expected there every hour   I am in hopes to make about 3000.$ out of this together with the flour adventure 2000.$ making 5000.$ I shall keep quiet for a few days in the arms of my dear wife in Monterey.

I am too much hurried to add more at present preparing to embark on board the Steamer for Monterey, I would not have you fail to write me by every steamer. direct your letters to Monterey Upper California

Your Affectionate Brother
J. H. Gleason

San Francisco   Jan 1, 1849 [1850]

Miss Frances A. Gleason, Plymouth, Mass.
My own dear Sister

Eleven weeks married & six weeks absent from my dear wife Kate, I left home (Monterey) on the 16th Nov'r & shall embark on board the steamer in two hours, & 9 hours passage will place me in the arms of one whom I love (pardon me) as well as my only sister Fanny, I have been quite a traveler since I left Monterey   I came up to Pueblo San Jose on horseback and reached this place by stage   I then took steam & have journeyed on the Sacramento, visiting Benicia & Sacramento City on my return about three weeks since   I left here for Monterey in a small schooner with about 20 passengers on board   we put out to sea & was obliged to return on account of the weather to Sausalito bay where we remained a few days riding out the storm. Beleiving that the vessel would have a long passage I hired a boat & men to take me to this place again & engaged my passage in the steamer with a determination never again to trust myself on board a sailing vessel.

The "California"[1] steamer arrived here day before yesterday. while I was on my way to the post office I met a youth who came up to me and took me by the hand & asked me if my name was Gleason. I replied in a most formal manner that I answered to that name. "Well" said he "contrasting my personal appearance with yours you may think it somewhat strange that I should take the liberty to salute respectability. however I call myself George Barnes and had the pleasure to see your sister & brothers about 40 days since when they were expecting you home every day." I immediately embraced my old schoolmate & made him overhawl his package of letters about 5,689 times, but nothing.

Barnes informed me that he was hard up & wished me to endeavour to "put him through" I said I would look about & if I could do anything for him I would be happy to do so. he is to call at my office soon. I have got him employment with a Dr Stokes who wants him to survey his farm and also examine his quick silver & copper mines, I mention this for the information of his parents which you will please advise them. I have met a number of my old schoolmates since I have been here & found them employment. I have sent John Spooner to Napa, & is a clerk with Thompson through my recommendation & influence.

You are expecting me home, — you must give up looking for me, I am sorry to say, my business is such that it is impossible for me to leave the country

---

[1] The *California* was the first of three side-wheel steamers built for the California trade by the Pacific Mail Steamship Company. She was the first steamship to navigate around South America, and was to meet the passengers from her sister ship the *Oregon,* who were coming across the Isthmus of Panama to avoid the long passage around the Horn. In the meantime gold had been discovered in California and passengers and ship got caught up in the frantic rush to the mines. The third ship was the *Panama.*

at present. it is true that I anticipated last summer a trip to the U.S. but it was for the purpose of purchasing a cargo of lumber but failing to bring the other parties to an agreement that were to be interested with me it was all "knocked in the head" had we succeeded in carrying it through we would have made 20,000.$ each.

I have not had a line from you since Aug't 13. you wrote then that Augustus was contemplating a voyage to California, if he is not already on his way & still persists in coming you must accompanying him & I will make provisions for your passage. I would not however advise anyone to come to California for a year or two yet untill the country is more settled a person who has employment at home should not leave it to journey this way. how many thousands have regreted the adventure.

In directing your letters to me, be careful to say *Monterey in large letters,* for the crowd is so great at San Fran'co office that a modest person is not able to get his letters for weeks after the steamer arrives. My love to Grandmother Aunt Cooper & Sylvia &c &c &c
      Your Affectionate Brother, James
P. S. Say to Caroline that I have not leisure to write by this boat, & Remember me to her dearly & her brother Ed. Always happy to hear from them, 40¢ postage is no consideration pile them up —
           J. H. G.

      San Francisco Mar 30 1850
My dear Father

We have had a most agreeable time since leaving Monterey my wife was not the least sea sick on board the steamer. she was on deck most of the time and as jovial as an old sea traveler   we are now living at Mr Green's and from the second story verandah we have a clear view of the City   the first night we arrived we went to the Circus, it being the farewell benefit of Foley   it was very good and Katie watched the feats of horsemanship in wonder.

The mortgage in question I have had recorded here and I find that you have the only mortgage on the property which gives you good security.

There is great excitement here about Trinidad Bay. a new gold region has been discovered up that way and expeditions are about starting for the new El Dorado. Brannan[2] is at the head of it and wherever he goes success attends him.

G —— has signed the obligation of Pachecoes and it is all right.

Catherine and myself unite in sending love to our parents & brothers & sisters.

Your Affectionate Son
Ja's H. Gleason

San Francisco   Mar 31, 1850

[To unidentified relative]

My dear Cousin

I have this day received your two letters by last steamer to your late husband and thinking that they might contain news of importance to your relatives here

---

[2] Sam Brannan, former leader of a group of Mormons, arrived aboard the *Brooklyn* in 1846 and had been the first excited courier announcing the discovery of gold as he rode from Sutter's Fort to San Francisco crying "Gold! Gold! Gold, from the American River!"

In 1847 the *Star* newspaper was first printed on a press brought by Brannan to California on the *Brooklyn*. As a man of influence and upright judgment, he was elected president of the Vigilantes in 1851. (Robert G. Cleland, *A History of California: The American Period*, N.Y., 1930, p. 297.)

Capt & myself opened them & by them we were informed of the death of Caroline   this is indeed hard for Edward & Caroline Augustus yet it is a consolation to know that they have grown up under the care of thier mother to an age when they can provide for themselves if necessary   she probably died with this feeling at her heart and if so she left the world happy & reconciled to her God who called her from us.   at the same time it is a consolation to know that neither brother or sister lived to mourn the loss of the other   it seems they both died the same month and while one steamer is bringing us the mournful intelegence of the one another steamer is conveying to us the sad news from home.

A part of your letter refers to Fanny, and it is the only news I have from her for months   you say that her health is much impaired, that she is depressed in spirits &c but that she is a lovely girl and you will take care of her.   this is indeed very kind in you to show so much warmth of feeling to one so dear to me as my Sister Fanny is. Whatever you may do to render her days happy and contented will surely be more appreciated by me than the highest favour shown to myself.

With sincerest sympathy for yourself, and my kindest regards to all my relatives and friends

     I am Your Affectionate Cousin
          Ja's H. Gleason

[To Miss Frances A. Gleason, Plymouth]
      San Francisco   Mar 31, 1850

My dear sister

You will see by the date of this that I am in San Francisco again. I arrived here from Monterey in the Steamer with my wife Catharine   it is the first time she was ever away from Monterey and you can imagine her surprise on arriving here after leaving so quiet a place as Monterey with regard to this place I may say that even New York itself would not create so much surprise in a person as this San Francisco you may pass by a vacant lot to day & in four days you will see a three story building upon it and occupied, this is no exageration. I am in San Francisco partly on a pleasure excursion & partly to arrange some business relating to the Estate of Wm. Paty I shall return to Monterey in the next Steamer which will be either on the 15th inst or 1st next month. I have no letters yet by this mail I presume they are at Monterey as I embarked on board the steamer before post office was oppened. I left orders to have the letters if any sent to me here & shall expect them soon. How is your treasury, do not fail to let me know when you are short of money and I will supply you I have not sent anything lately owing to the heavy pressure of the money market it has been impossible to make any collections for the last two mo's and then my lumber loss about $4000. slap out of pocket has rather pressed me, however I shall soon recover and be flush. I shall endeavour to send you something by Mrs Paty who will depart for the U. States the 15th or 1st My wife tells me to say that as she cannot write in English you must excuse her and as a token of her deep affection for her sister Fanny she will send a pina scarf by Mrs Paty it is something I never saw at home and I cannot say how it will be appreciated but it is enough to say that they are valued here at 125.$ each. She will also send her Deguerotype in her bridal dress and reclining on a harp as she was at a moment on the marriage eve, when my attention was called to her. I can hardly account for not receiving your Deguerotype so long as I have looked for it, what can it mean. I do not believe that it is not with me because you have grown ugly for my friend tell me you are beautiful. I have my Grandmother's in Monterey and I worship it.

Please remember me to all my relatives and friends,
Your Affectionate Brother
James

San Francisco   July 1. 1850

My dear sister Fanny

I am again in San Fran'co having arrived here a few days since in the steamer & take the steamer to day for Monterey.   the object of my present visit to this place has been to purchase goods for my store in Monterey & to negociate for the sale of land in Sacramento City on a/c of the Estate of our lamented Uncle William. I shall be in Monterey early tomorrow morning when I am assured I shall find a letter from you. I took from the Post Office yesterday a number of letters for John who has left with his family for Oahu.   he, alone, will return immediately to the coast.

I have a great desire to go home but it seems that every month I remain here plunges me still deeper in business.   since my last to you I have received the Agency of the "Empire City Line" of steamers for Monterey & this together with my commercial affairs & the settlement of Williams Estate keeps my time constantly occupied   however I am determined to make a visit home within six months at all hazards, & then I will bring you to my home in California. I left my wife well at Monterey & should nothing occur to frustrate the workings of nature I shall be a father in a few months, and then I am going home partly to see my old acquaintences and relations & partly to get clear of a squalling baby. I like babys very much but not untill they arrive at a certain age. I forwarded you by Mr Barnes a few weeks ago my wife's Deguerotype likeness & also a Pina scarf a present from my wife & she wants you to send her in return some baby's fixings made by your own hands.

An idea has just struck me. I will write to Teschmacher an esteemed friend in whom I can place every confidence & should you desire you can come out here with him   we look for him in about 4 mo's he will give you what funds you may want, And now I shall close with a *demand* for you to embark with him. Coz Martha Ann can advise you what clothing you may want for the voyage. I know that nothing prevents your coming.   let not your affection for Agustus detain you   you can marry well & marry into wealth in California.

I have every confidence in seeing you now in about 4 mo's in the embrace of my dear wife & your brother who loves you so dearly. Call & see my old friend Tho's O. Larkin before you leave   I believe he is now in Boston.

Give my love to my brothers, Grandmother, Sylvia, Edward, & Caroline &c. &c.

I shall try to write to John & Herbert if I get time.
Your Affectionate Brother
James

[To Miss Frances A. Gleason, Plymouth]
Monterey   July 31, 1850
My dear Sister

Your valued favour of 13th May is before me, I am happy to hear that you were well. You thank me for my liberal present to you — you owe me no thanks, it is a duty and also a source of heartfelt pleasure to know that

I am able to make you comfortable   if money & my affections can accomplish it as long as I have a dollar my brothers & sisters shall not want. Had it not been my misfortune to loose $7000, at one sweep last winter I would have made you a visit long ere this, & it this reason that I have not sent you anything lately as I have been obliged to borry funds at an enormous interest to meet certain adventures that I had entered upon. My father in law was speaking to me a few days since about an adventure to the U.S. next spring   he will advance 20,000$ & if I can settle up & raize about 10,000.$ cash I shall be in the U.S. by next April purchasing a cargo for California market. I do not wish you to place any confidence in my coming, and perhaps be disappointed for something else may capsize the plan, yet I am very anxious to go home and shall try all in my power to get away.

I have built me a snug cottage in Monterey adjoining my store and have a spare room furnished for you as soon as you wish to ocupy it   I shall expect you out here by the last of August.   hoping you have availed yourself of the opp'y offered by my friend Teschmacher.

My wife tells me that I shall be a father in about 6 or 8 weeks, of course she ought to know. I've nothing more to say about it.

You say that you have not rec'd any letters from me for some months   I have made it a point to write the 1st of every month & if they have not come to hand they have been lost or mislaid. Your letters have come very regular   I get one from you I beleive every month.

I am Expecting Capt Paty daily from the Sandwich Islands. I think he will leave his family there as they are more comfortable at Oahu than they could possibly be on California.

Hoping to hear from you again soon I must close with my love to Grandmother Sylvia, Cousins &c
Your Affectionate Brother
James

[pr Steamer]
Monterey   Aug 31. 1850
To Miss Frances A. Gleason, Plymouth
My Dear Sister

Your valued favours of 10th July & 15th May were both received yesterday by mail from San Francisco together with numerous other letters from John, Herbert, Caroline, Sylvia and Coz Martha Ann. I have not time to answer them all by this steamer but in the meanwhile I beg you will tender them my warmest thanks for their kind notice of me & say I will write them in due time. My last to you was dated Aug 1st from San Francisco & on my absence from this City my friends elected me Alderman,   just fancy me an alderman a young stripling weighing about 125 lbs   my friends tell me I must eat about ten pound of food daily for about a month so as to get up a corperation & bear the appearance of so dignified an office.

I am pleased to learn of the safe arrival at your hands of the Deguerotype likeness & scarf sent by Kate. I read in Spanish your letter to her & she thinks you flatter her too much & where you say you are "decidedly plain" she says how can a young lady write so pretty a letter & be "plain"   it would'nt go down with her,   she is very anxious for your likeness.

It is 10 Oc at night & I have to arise early in the morning & ride horseback about 60 miles on business therefore I shall drop this at once & drop myself into

bed with Kate who is lying by me with her shoulders uncovered in all the beauty of her own dear self.
    Good Night As ever Affectionate
               James
Dont forget me to Grandmother and all her children & acquaintances

---

         Monterey Sept. 30. 1850.
To Miss Frances A. Gleason, Plymouth
Beloved Sister

 Your valued letter dated at Pittsfield was received a few days since and I was much pleased to learn that you was on a tour into the country. you are now probably while I am writing this arriving at your home in Plymouth as your letter tells me you will return about the last of this month. I hope you have not admitted anything to pass you that would add to your pleasure & comfort which money can purchase. Whatever expense you have incurred on your journey I will settle as I get an opportunity to remit you. I will not fail to send you some money by the next steamer, that leaves in 15 days.

 I have strong ideas now of going home, I was thinking it over yesterday afternoon at the dinner table near my wife "Why do you look so sad" she says, and her words aroused me to a sence of my position. I recollect I was pricking the outside of a watermellon with a fork with my head down and had been silent for some length of time. thus run my thoughts — suppose I were to leave in the next steamer for the U.S. — how can I manage my business — cannot leave my partner in charge for he has not the energy to carry it on — it will go to the d — l if I leave it with him — put every thing up at Auction — it will only be sacraficed — not bring cost

Monterey Sept. 30. 1850.

To Miss Frances A. Gleason,
Plymouth

Beloved Sister

Your valued letter dated at Pittsfield was received a few days since and I was much pleased to learn that you was on a tour into the country. you are now probably while I am writing this arriving at your home in Plymouth as your letter tells me you will return about the last of this month. I hope you have not admitted anything to pass you that would

Miss Frances A. Gleason
Plymouth
Mass.

A PORTION OF JAMES GLEASON'S LETTER TO HIS BELOVED SISTER,
OF SEPTEMBER 30, 1850, WITH ITS ADDRESSED SELF COVER

— good prospect of making $5000. during the winter — if I go home spend 2 or 3000.$ — difference in pocket of 8000.$ — ten years from home — by thunder how will I feel again in Plymouth. I must go — I will go — I can leave my wife at her fathers — I can put 2000.$ in my pocket — I can sell off my stock of goods within a month — I can rent out my premises for the winter, & I can get my ticket — jump on board, and off she paddles — here is a damper — arriving in the U.S. in the middle of winter — why I would freeze to death surely. —

Here you have a train of my present thoughts. I am in a perfect quandary what to do. It is possible that I may jump on board of the November boat & be with you in December yet it is barely possible for I would wish be at home in the Spring which I shall certainly effect if I do not go before.

The City assessor handed me to day my bill of taxes & I find my property in California is valued at about 25,000.$ which I have to pay taxes on this year. I wish I could be certain that I am worth this amt. but my property is so mixed up that I can hardly realize it.

Your Affectionate Brother
James

[pr Steamer "Oregon" cover address:
Mrs. Martha Ann Paty, Plymouth, Mass., U.S.A.]

Monterey Dec. 1. 1850
To Miss Frances A. Gleason, Plymouth
My Beloved Sister

The "Oregon" will be here tomorrow morn on her way to Panama & I will devote a this evening in writing home.

I have no letter from you since your return from

Pittsfield yet I am in hopes to get them tomorrow by the steamer for it so happens at times that Monterey letters are taken by mistake to San Francisco and some ten days passes after their arrival on the coast before they reach us. I received by last steamer which arrived on the 20th Nov'r a letter from Coz Martha Ann & one from Herbert of 28 pages of Philosophical and moral matter (how he has changed) together with Deguerotype likenesses of our good mother and himself. I was very much pleased to get them. I also wish I was as good a looking fellow as he is & knew half as much. However I've got a boy that I'm proud of born on the 31st of October makes him one month old. We have given him the name of Henry. the name is short and in Spanish it sounds sweet Henrique. At his birth we did not weigh him but we supposed to weigh about 10 pounds. you can see the Paty stick out in him at every point. only a month old his large bright blue eyes flash and sparkle like a metior and his pretty little mouth will at times curl itself into a smile so cunningly that I would give anything to have you by. Catharine says that he is to large for her to take care of & in a few years he will be strong enough to master his father & advises me to ship him off in the next steamer to you.

I still have in view my journey to the U. States next spring. I am advised that March is the best month for embarking from here, the only thing that has prevented my being at home now is the heavy loss I met with in a lumber speculation of $7000. in clear cash at one sweep which has considerably embarassed my business. I have valuable property yet but mostly in real estate & I cannot at present realize from it. I am at present borrowing money at a heavy interest but expect soon to be out of debt.

Martha Ann writes that she has advanced you $119.62¢   I will without fail send you by next steamer 2, or 300.$ so as to enable you to repay her & have some on hand   I was surprised to hear that the expenses of your trip was so light   I expected it would be at least $300. Martha Ann was very kind to advance you the amount.   she says that you have funds in Uncle Samuell hands.   you ought not to let your money go out of your hands.   keep what I send you in your own private draw. & then when you need it you always have it.   the interest you may obtain for it at home is too trivial to loan it out. I shall make it a point to send you a small amount by every month after I recover my business again. I must close this now for I have a number of letters to write yet to night.

Remember me affectionately to Father Grandmother Sylvia John & Herbert, Caroline & Edward. I may write to each of them yet by this steamer.

I want my *fathers* likeness & *your own*   never mind if you are thin.   we will have another when you get stout.

Your Affectionate Brother — James

Monterey   March 3d 1851

To Miss Frances A. Gleason, Plymouth

My Dear Sister

We are in possession of your kind letter of Dec'r 10th and the box of valuables, the little dresses are supurb — the neck scarf is just to my taste, the little shirt from the hands of Coz Martha Ann was unfolded & tossed about by the shoulders before the admiring crowd of relatives. I pitched immediately upon the miniatures & I must confess my weakness. I could not restrain the tears as I gazed & gazed again upon the likeness, there were the same features & the same expression so long lost to my view. Johnny shows nobly on plate, my wife asked why such good looking men never come to California prehaps if I were to dress up I could make very near as good a figure.   there would be but one thing wanting — that is the whiskers. I will tell you how I dress — I have on at the present moment a slouched hat something like this [small sketch of the hat] a green baize jacket cod-roy (If I have spelled it right) pants, a pair of pegged thick sole boots, and a cotton handkf in my pocket.   when I go home you will find me in about the same style of dress. I am trying all in my power to bring my affairs into a focus so as to enable me to make a visit home.   our San Francisco Agent for the Empire City Line paid us a visit a few days since.   he stopped at our house   he offered me a passage home free but it is impossible for me to leave at present   I will tell you how I stand

1st   I have a law suit coming off in April   the Point Pinos case in which I am interested $8000.

2d   I have on hand about $4000. worth of merchandise which I am anxious to close off & cannot do it at once unless at a great sacrafice.

3d   I am owing to sundry individuals about $5000.

4   I have about $5000.$ in debts which I alone can attend to.

This is about the substance of my future six months labour before me. However I am desperate to get home. Since receiving the likenesses I have been exceedingly home sick, *first time for ten years*   I have now made up my mind to leave here in May at the fartherest. they must something extraordinary turn up to delay me beyond that time.

I thank Johnny for his kind letter and will answer it by next steamer.   he seems sadly disappointed by my not sending him funds   he should take into consideration that since promising him the means to enable him to establish himself in business, that I have suffered severe losses. I am about $15,000, poorer than I was this day last year   had it not been fore these sucessive & severe losses I would long ere this been among you.

Our little Henrique is in fine health and growing rapidly   we feed him on beef-steak [five months old!] poor little fellow got a peice down his throat the other day & it came very near making a finish of him. he sported yesterday one of the dresses in question   I appeared also in the new cravat   I laboured for two hours tying the bow & had to give it up untill Kate came home from church & she done the thing up perfectionately as we say or tyduated it good.   she joins me in love to all our New England relatives,

Your Beloved & home sick Brother
James

[Steamer "Northern"]

Monterey   May 15, 1851

To Miss Frances A. Gleason, Plymouth
My Dear Sister

Your valued letter of March quien sabe what date came safely to hand and while I give you many thanks, hope you will continue punctual in writing although I may not answer by every mail. Am happy to hear of the payment of the draft for $200. remitted by T. H. Green & hope this will enable you to "keep up appearances" untill I am somewhat released from my present pecuniary embarrassment when I will remit again.

Myself & wife think that we have the finest boy that could possibly be manafactured, he is only six months old and we feed him on slops if you know what that is and at times we find him knawing away at a peice of beef with right good relish, he is just commencing to crawl and never cries which makes him the more interesting. he has a smile for every one at any time. Cradles are not known in this part of the world, I'll tell you how we or rather how my wife manages. A peice of cord is stretched from one bed post to the other so as to swing loose, then a blanket is folded over the cord and opened by two sticks one at the head and one at the foot just wide enough to admit the little cherub, and this is the way we swing him to sleep. It would please you more to see the little fellow in his bath-tub he enjoys it so much spattering the water with his hands and jumping about in it as though it was his only true element.

My wife spends the most of her time in the garden where I left her about ten minutes since loosening the earth around the "sweet Williams." by the way that reminds me of my Cousin Bill whom I had nearly forgotten give him my cariño when you meet him Kate wants some flower seeds, good & fresh ones are rarely to be obtained here & you will confer an everlasting pleasure & favour on her by selecting & forwarding some rare ones. she is down with me ever since we received your likeness. she often asks me how I had the shame to send her ugly phiz among my beautiful & accomplished relatives she thinks that Johnny must be a noble fellow.

About going home — what shall I say? You cannot be more anxious to have me among you than I am to vamos. I am sometimes inclined to budge on the instant, and then all at once an overruling consideration holds me back & then again Kate "says you shall not go" or in her own words "no ti vagas" but I will go & cannot say when.

San Francisco is in ruins destroyed by fire on the 4th inst.   loss supposed about 30 millions, the most beautiful & wealthy portion of the city is gone.   sometimes I think that my fortune was somewhat favoured by my selling out there & settling here   there has been over half a million of property burnt over the land I once owned there & had I improved it myself I would have been one of the sufferers.   at the late fire the ashes of the once beautiful buildings "Union Hotel & Parker House" lay over the same land   they cost over 200,000.$ You will see particulars of this in the papers, therefore I'll close the details.

Tell Coz Martha Ann that I have not heard from Uncle John for nearly two months   he is in San Francisco & I suppose he keeps her informed about her husbands affairs, as he is there on the spot.

Give my love to all — have not room on this sheet to mention names.

    Your Affec't Brother James

       Monterey January 1 1852
To Miss Frances A. Gleason, Plymouth, Mass.
Beloved Sister

Your two kind letters of Aug 24 & Oct. 24 came duly to hand and I am ashamed at not having answered them before.   the only excuse I have to offer is that I have no excuse whatever. I must plead criminal by not having the politeness even to acknowledge the receipt of your valuable present the box of flower seeds that came to hand in such perfect order. My wife was pleased almost beyond conception and sends you mil gracias por su bondad. she is in her bed yet not having fully recovered from her confinement, she presented me on the 13th December with a little daughter which we have named Lucia or Lucy in English   I like the name mostly for its shortness.   we thought of naming her Fanny but reconsidered the question and came to the conclusion that there were too many Fanny's among our relatives already. I send enclosed her hair with some of Henrique's also.

I am happy to learn that you are recovering your health.

I intended to write you a long letter when I commenced this, but I have a severe headache and am obliged to close abruptly. this is the 12th page I have written tonight   the steamer will be in early in the morning and only remains a few moments.

Give my best love to Grandmother John & Herbert Sylvia Aunt Cooper Caroline & Edward &c &c &c

My wife send her love

Good bye with a happy New Year

Your Affectionate Brother
James

Monterey   January 15, 1852
To Miss Frances A. Gleason, Plymouth
Affectionate Sister

My last was under date Jan. 1, 1852   since then matters have trotted along with me about the same. Little Lucia is our pet now & is as charming as a good turtle soup or a plate of oysters. Henrique is by my side kicking up considerable excitement because the

Letters from Monterey, 1850-1859

nurse delays bringing in his dinner   I think he will be some pumpkins when he has a few more years on his head   he can fight now when there is cause.

The "Golden Gate" came into our port yesterday bring receipts from New York in 21 days the quickest trip on record with 1300 passengers on board   most every one in Mont'y got letters but me   a friend of mine rec'd a letter from Buffalo in less than a month when two months had always been the time for his communications to arrive from that place.

I am about starting for San Fran'co by land   I am only waiting for company for it is yet somewhat dangerous to travel the road alone   I expect to be off within three days.   the principal object of this trip to see about the estate of our late Uncle Wm.

My wife has fully recovered from her late confinement and is now out in the garden trimming flowers she cannot read English and I am too lazy to ensenarla I have just called her to tell her of the comparisons I made regarding Lucia and she inquired if I always wrote such trash home & to write something sensible. you would be highly amused to look in upon us when I get a letter from you.   she will take the letter and studdy out every word with the help of a dictionary she has not confidence in my translations for she has caught me several times cheating her.

In a few years we will have a fine orchard of fruit trees.   we have now forty set out and growing finely. we put into the ground a few days since some of the flower seeds you were so kind to send us   it may seem strange to you to sow in January but it is always warm weather with us,
    I must close Give My Love to all
        Your Affectionate Brother
          James

P. S.

I have this moment on the point of closing this been handed your letter of Nov'r 25 just arrv'd by mail. Uncle John has not yet arrived from China. I will on his arrival give the earliest attention to the matter our grandmother desires.

Then Carrie is married. God bless the dear kind soul.   how I wish to see her, give her my kind love and also my new relative her husband Edwin

Yours &c   James

[Courtesy of Capt Baker]
San Francisco   January 29, '52
To Miss Frances A. Gleason, Plymouth
My dear Sister

I arrived here a few days since by land and depart for Monterey tomorrow. I have nothing of interest to communicate. Capt Baker sails immediately for the U. States and I regret much my inability to remit you some cash by him, it being so excellent an opportunity. I have been greatly disappointed here in not collecting sundry A/c's which have been due to me for a long while. I shall however send you some money as soon as it is in my power.

Hurry father's likeness along   I am very anxious to see it.

Love to all   Your Affectionate Brother
James

Monterey   March 15, 1852
To Miss Frances A. Gleason, Plymouth
My Dear Sister

Since my last I have nothing worthy to communicate,

I am still in Monterey with my family and getting along comfortably, the little children Lucia & Henrique are growing up finely and I feel quite proud of them. Henrique has just learned to walk and he is on his feet continually.

We have just received melancholly news from the Sacramento the city has been inundated completely and upwards of 300 lives lost. I fear this will ruin the city completely.

Uncle John has arrived from China and is now in San Francisco I have not received a letter from him but expect to in the mail to night   it is supposed that he will do well on the voyage when every thing is wound up.

My wife joins me in love to all particularly Grandmother.

                                    Your Affectionate Brother
Want of time makes me brief   James

                    San Francisco   Nov'r 29, 1852
To Miss Frances A. Gleason, Plymouth
My dearly beloved sister

Since my last to you I have become quite a wanderer I have been in the mountains several months catching wild horses and hunting bears and visited the following places San Luis, San Miguel San Juan San Jose Martinez Benecia Colusa Munroeville, Placerville, Tehema Sacramento City and now I am found in San Francisco after a five months round and a very happy adventure. I shall probably be with my family in a few days at the farm   they are all well the last I heard from them and thriving finely.   little Henrique is growing up fast and can now talk and assert his rights. O[ur little] Lucia is a choice bud she is [the pet of] the whole family   how you wo[uld be ple]ased to see her.

Uncle John is n[ow here   he] arrived a few days ago from the [islands as mas]ter of the Brig "Baltimore" and is to leave Tuesday on the return trip   he is looking as well as I ever saw him.   little Johnny is also with him   I was surprised to find him grown up so tall   he had entirely forgotten me.

I was at Sacramento City the day after the great fire and it was the most melancholly sight I ever witnessed, to see thousands without a home and even without a shelter to escape from the heavy three days rain that followed after the city was in ruins.[3]

I am in hopes when I get home to find some letters from the atlantic states for I have not heard from you for some months and I am anxious to hear how you get along. I have been in the woods so long that I have almost forgotten how to write   in our hunt we saw twenty five bears, killed one that weighed about 500 lbs and caught five horses.

This much for the present with my love to all.
Yours very affectionately
Santiago
P. S.   My love [portion cut out] & Grandmother

Monterey   Feb. 15, 1853
To Miss Frances A. Gleason, Plymouth, Mass
My beloved Sister

I have not heard from home for eight or nine months and I cannot account for this silence. I have written to you several times and have received no answer. I have

---

[3] The fire which gutted Sacramento in 1852 was of incendiary origin, trash blazes flaring up while others were being fought. The suffering of the homeless people was augmented by the flooding of the Sacramento River.

been roaming all over California during the last six months and now find myself again in Monterey. I had a very serious time of it the months of November and December at the farm of my father in law where my family are still remaining   a traveller arrived there having the small-pox and after ten days sickness he died amongst the family,   every precaution was taken to clean the house afterwards by burying and burning everything that came in contact with the disease but to no avail   in about eight or ten days the disease broke out among the family and there were eleven sick at one time   myself and my two sisters in law escaped and we were completely worn out with fatigue   I was almost continually day and night administering medicines   my wife was sick only with the fever and soon recovered   my little boy had been vaccinated and escaped but my little Lucia took it severely and suffered for two weeks exceedingly. I feared that she would be marked in the face but to our infinate pleasure I find it has left her without a sign and as beautiful cheerful and playful as ever   she is the pet of the whole family and I fear her grandmother will spoil her by too much indulgence. Little Henrique is the finest little boy out of jail, he is very forward of his age and his parents (of course) believe he will make a smart man   his main ambition at the present day is to throw the lasso over the dogs and lambs and throw them down as the rancheros do the cattle. I left my family a few days ago and am here putting my house in order to receive them   it has been closed for six months and requires some time to clean it. I should have mentioned while I was on the subject that each one that was sick recovered and none were marked but an indian servant girl,   it is impossible for me to describe to you in words the distress beneath that roof about Christmas time and the anxiety felt by the sick and well. I had never been amongst it before and not having been vaccinated since my infancy (in Sandwitch which I recollect perfectly well for I was frightened nearly out of my juvenile sences). I felt almost sure of taking it being continually by the bedside and walking the room for hours together with my little Lucia   the poor little infant was blind for three days and nights at the time the disease had reached its height.   should I live a hundred years the moment she opened her eyes would be fresh in my memory   she extended her little hands towards me and seemed to feel so glad to see me that I could not leave her a moment for the whole day. I had before given up all hopes of saving her, partly from the circumstance of my father in law telling me that I must be prepared to loose her for she could not live   and when she opened her eyes and appeared so cheerful and called for her playthings I could not restrain the gush of tears that started from my eyes.   she is dearer to me now than ever.

The probability is that should no accident interfere with the workings of nature I will have an addition to my family in about four months.   is it possible I am so "adelantade" in domestic affairs I can hardly realise it, for it appears to me I am nothing but a boy yet "sic transit gloria mundi."

How is my dear grandmother?   does she enjoy yet good health?   and my kind father and brothers how are they all?   more than eight months since I have heard from my atlantic home, perhaps I am forgotten — "quien sabe" Notwithstanding give them my kind love, and believe myself and wife to entertain everlasting and true afection for them, & Yourself

Santiago

Please do write [this in large handwriting]

San Benito Rancho   January 1, 1855[4]

My Dear Sister

Here I am once more in the interior at the farm of my father in law with all my family around me save my wife and youngest child.   they being at Monterey. I came here to spend Christmas and New Years with the old folks,   they must have all their relatives with them at Christmas   my father in law one of the old fashion Eng. Gentlemen cannot of course forget the old Custom, and a delightful time we have had for the last week the house crowded with guests from all parts of the country   Turkeys — plum puddings — roast pigs — music — dancing — bull fighting and racing continually kept up with a perfect looseness   this day finishes the feast and tomorrow hurrah for home. My wife was confined on the 30th of November and on that day I became father to my fourth child all in healthy & promising condition and smart as steel traps. I can hardly realize the fact. I left my wife eight days ago and she was regaining her health rapidly   she had then risen from her bed and taking her usual rounds about the house. I shall be with her in four or five days. I have purchased a fine carriage and my brother in law Tom presented me with a span of white poneys, lively fellows they are and they take me too & fro flying. I always manage to visit the old folks at least once in two months and remain several days they are very much attached to me. I regret that my wife is not here to our merry christmas and you also, how delighted you would be among us   you would enjoy your life so pleasantly.   to be sure you would find the manners and customs entirely different from what you are accus-

---

[4] Beginning with this date apparently envelopes were used for mailing the letters, as the addressed self cover no longer appears. The same occurred with five scattered earlier letters after 1848.

tomed too but at the same time you would find them to your taste. give me the harp and guitar for music in preference to your piano or Boston Brigade or Brass Bands and for song what is there more sweet than a spanish song they are still singing in my ears while I am writing this and I am sure the girls are singing now in the ante chamber while I have stowed myself away in the fartherest corner of the house to give my thoughts to thee so as not to be disturbed fearing that if I do not write now I shall not have time to write after arriving at Monterey to send by next mail The songsters I think are in the sala and they are singing one of my old favourite songs "El Relampago" ["Flash of Lightning"]. I have discontinued writing for a few moments to listin, and lit one of my Manilas No 3 thrown myself back in the rocking chair and swinging too and fro occasionally sipping my sherry which stands at my elbow in a wine glass which perhaps might have been manufactured for all that I know in the Sandwich glass factory, that is the glass, the wine I am certain came from Europe the cigars are some of my old stock brought over from the Islands in 1846 I only "bring them out" on certain occasions and keep ordinary cigars for my friends. age gives a peculiar virtue to good wine and cigars. I have both and I am very saving with them for they have both nearly given out and when they do I shall most probably set aside smoking and drinking, that is for awhile, untill I can replenish. I have some thoughts of taking to a pipe. I feel myself now aproaching old age [he was then 32 years of age!] or to that point when a man feels little inclined to hard work I am very fond of laying by and see others work but not disposed to lend a hand myself. It does me good to see the old Governor manage, gets up in the morning with the sun (a habit which I have not as yet got accustomed to) and if the feild labourers are not at their duties at time they are very likely to be hurried up with the old hickory cane which the old gentleman has continually at his side or behind the dining-room door.   he then then takes his usual morning round down to the feild remains there untill nine when all hands are called to breakfast, some fifteen or twenty of them   Breakfast being over at it again and the old bos coolly takes his forenoon smoke at that old stinking pipe   If I smoke a pipe it shall be a clean one at least   the old fellow puffs away at least two hours on a streatch when he gets started but then he does not smoke strong tobacco. We have dinner at One and lounge untill three   that is the working men I lounge all day, being here on a visit,   tomorrow I am for a hunt which now reminds me that I ought to be at work now cleaning out my gun, but however I will have plenty of time in the evening but I am getting off the track.   the days work being over all assemble in the large hall around that large old fashion fire place being 6½ feet wide 5 ft high & 2 ft deep (it is a fact) and I dare say it consumes in cold weather a large wagon load of wood each day   now and then out comes the guitar   almost every one plays and all dance — sometimes play whist and others of more sober turn lounge about corners of the room reading or looking on, and the old lady & Gentleman sitting in the corner of the fire place the latter continually smokeing and spitting at the embers and chatting and spinning his old yarns with some new guest   at nine O.c generally the old folks go off to bed and leave the feild clear for the youngsters to have a general good time. this is our life at the rancho and a merry life it is. every once in two weeks we have a rodeo, buqueros all turn out to herd the cattle on the rodeo ground so that they cannot stray afar off, every hill and vally is to be traveled over on the farm to collect them   this is fine sport for me always having a fine horse under me   we have a rodeo day after tomorrow, about 1500 head of Cattle & 100 head of horses & mares [portion of letter burned away, a few words of five lines missing].

[I mus]t close this now for it is getting [late] and I can hardly see to write [   ]y it aside for continuance [   ] you at the same time (which [   ] nearly forgotten) a happy New Year.

January 2d — Rainy day — all ready for the hunt and compelled to stay within doors.   have been laying off before a cheerful fire reading I. K. Marvins "Reveries of a Bachelor" a most capital work — get it and read it. I think it very interesting. I have turned over nearly every thing in the house to find some letter paper and without success   this is the best and I had to steal it from the segar maker and answers very well, in the absence of better — just got news from Monterey — Wife & little Francisca (who I have named after you) are well and my wife chides me for remaining here so long and I have only been here ten days   she has heard of your marriage and as soon as there is any thing in the wind she wants you to advise her so as to send a present.

Good bye for awhile   Your Affectionate Brother
                                                        James

I gave this to a friend to mail and he forgot to do so and I have just found out the fact (Jan'y 29th) and have opened it to explain   G. ——

                            Monterey   June 14th 1856
To Mrs Frances Tribble[5]   Plymouth
My dear Sister

With me there has been but little change since my last letter home save I am so many months older & apparently no better nor wiser than I then was   I occupy the same position, office hours from 10 to 12 & 2 to 4 and outside of these most of the time out riding in the woos, lounging about the house or at work in the garden, occasionally light a segar go down town and "put some one through" or get put through myself at billiards a game I am passionately fond of and the only game I indulge in, fifteen years experience has rendered me quite an expert player. My family affairs go on delightfully, all in the best of health, Kate is one of the best of wifes always cheerful gay & loving and the babies full of fun & mischief. Henrique is now quite a youngster, he sails his kite & drives his hoop equal to any of them. I think his mother keeps him cleaner than I used to be at his age   you never see him in the dirt and he is most decidedly opposed going to school without first being certain of having a white handkerchief in his pocket — Lucia is growing up quite pretty, tall and slender and has a modest but intelligent look, Marianita is more of the ranchero build robust & stout she is the most healthy of all the rest, having lived on the farm since she was born where milk is fresh & abundant and fresh fat beef at all times. there is no food so delicious to my taste as the ribs of a young steer thrown on the coals when newly killed. Fanny has your features to perfection, she is now just commencing to walk & she affords us considerable amusement so very

---

[5] The only one of the preserved letters to be addressed to his sister using her married name.

cunning & knowing. My wife is now about being confined again Heavens! what shall I do with so many babies in less than a fortnight they will call me father of five children   Mr Hartnell an old resident of this place & now in his grave was one day asked how many children he had.   his reply was, twenty one in all but thank God half of them died young otherwise they would all have been beggars. Now God forbid that such an unholy sentiment as this should fasten upon me. I cannot beleive that he ever made the remark for he was a very good man & a particular friend of mine & I knew him long and well but such is the story they tell of him. I think when a man has five children to feed clothe and educate it is full time for him to abandon the thought of adding more unless he has the resources of a Rothchild to back him. It is astonishing what effect this climate has on the female as soon as she is married, they all have babies — every one of them, and they keep having them at least one in every twelve months as long as they live unless they live to be very old or thier husbands die, why confound it ladies born in the East & lived in the Eastern states for years in the happy bonds of matrimony who never had a child & lost the hopes of having any have arrived on our shores and all at once they swell out like old Falstaff and the next thing Papa is in a state of extacy and delight   If I thought it would have the reverse effect by taking my wife to the atlantic shores I would be tempted to undertake it, so much for family matters.

You will see through the columns of our papers that San Francisco is in a state of revolution   the greater and better portion of the citizens about 6000 strong have enrolled themselves under the banner of the vigilance committee and are in arms against the constitution   they now are so well organized that they have the ruling power & nothing but U.S. forces can break them up   the victims that fall into thier hands undergo a regular trial & have the priveledge of counsel and as they are tried they are either banished or hung according to the degree of the crime   the Governor has issued his Proclamation to the effect of maintaining law & order & calling upon all good citizens of the State for support but it apparantly has no more effect than the idle wind.   should he succeed however in enrolling a sufficient number to warrant an attack with success he may issue his orders and there would be much blood shed or the Committee quietly dissolve.   the strength of the Committee is based on this, they have brought to light the fact and clearly proven it up that nearly all the State and County officers of San Francisco hold thier places by virtue of illegal voting and ballot box stuffing at the last gen'l election and this Committee have under these circumstances already demanded a portion of them to resign, and should they fail to do so it is authentically reported that the Executive Committee will banish them   W. T. Sherman Major Gen'l resigned a few days ago, but it was a voluntary act, under a full conviction as he says that the voting was a fraud upon the people and he desires no office of trust unless it is clothed with punity.

It is difficult to conceive how all this will terminate, it may be in a civil war and it may gradually die away if all is left to the Committee   it is between them and the Governor   the latter has only to issue his order at any moment and in an instant the thouroughfares of San Francisco will be bathed in blood friends and relatives in "one red burial blent"   the Committee are strong and powerful composed of resolute and determined men the flower of the State and they proclaim that they will hold their ground at the hazzard of thier lives & fortunes and oppose all opposition most strenuously and fearlessly untill they have finished thier finished thier [*sic*] investigations — punished the guilty, and purified San Francisco.

I only make these few remarks upon the present state of affairs leaving you to gather from the daily papers a more general and full history of the present & past times which you will indeed find very interesting commencing from the assasination of Gen'l Richardson & following that of Mr King & the execution of Cora & Casey. it will of course not be so exciting to you as to us surrounded by all these unhappy outbreaks. business is almost completely suspended, and a feverish exitement prevails in every part of the state among all classes wondering what the next move may be and who the next victim for banishment or the gallows.[6]

---

[6] Many of the disastrous fires in San Francisco were supposed to have been kindled for the opportunities of plundering by lawless elements of the Barbary Coast, which thrived except for occasional setbacks resulting from outbursts of civic virtue. The end came in 1851 when an earthquake shook down the flimsy thing and clean flame did the rest.

If the duly appointed sources of justice became inadequate beyond endurance, the citizens of San Francisco had a habit of taking matters into their own hands. In 1851, at the instigation of Sam Brannan, there were a few justified hangings and many deportations, causing a scarcity of "coves" and a corresponding sense of security and order to prevail for a time. Then crooked politics, another form of toxin which had infected the city administration, culminated in the murders of William Richardson, W. S. Marshall and James King, founder and editor of the *Bulletin*. It was said that there had been 1400 murders in San Francisco during its first seven years as an American city and only one lawful execution. So again the bell on the firehouse tolled the summons for justice.

William T. Coleman, the man of the hour, was chosen leader, and the organization grew to number 3500. Five companies of the National Guard disbanded and threw their strength with the Vigilantes. When all was in readiness a ring of determined men surrounded the jail and demanded the custody of the two murderers, Charles Cora and James Casey. A cannon pointed at the big door convinced the sheriff and also Governor J. N. John-

this is quite an elaborate instrument of writing for me and I believe I will close with this page and write again here after but you must promise me truly to reply to this   the last two letters from me to you a long

---

son, who was present, that it would be better to lend moral support and that resistance would be unwise. Mayor Van Ness and William T. Sherman, then Adjutant-General of California, were helpless onlookers as the prisoners were hastened to the stronghold of the Vigilantes. This was a two story building on Sacramento Street with a breastwork of sand-bags ten feet high and six feet thick. This was called "Fort Gunnybags." A swift but a fair trial and a double lynching preceded a general clean-up of undesirables. Every ship that left the harbor carried away a few unwilling passengers.

The schooner *Julia* surreptitously left Benicia with six cases of muskets intended for the state armory, where 300 troops were housed, but the vessel was intercepted at San Pablo and the guns landed at Fort Gunnybags. A so-called Law and Order Committee had organized to oppose the Vigilantes and had loaded the *Julia*. All military and state officials adopted a policy of hands off and this attitude extended even to the President of the United States.

The one exception was Judge Terry of the Supreme Court. He blustered down from Sacramento but his ardor cooled when he found the trend of public opinion. However he chanced to witness the arrest of a relative in connection with the *Julia* affair and stepped in to interfere. During the scuffle he stabbed the arresting officer and then, in spite of his rotundity, made good speed to the Armory and slammed the door after him. The bell on the fort called out the now five thousand Vigilantes who surrounded the Armory with military precision and wheeled cannon into position. The defenders readily capitulated and this netted the committee three hundred muskets and much ammunition. Judge Terry took up rather confined quarters at Fort Gunnybags while all waited breathlessly the outcome of the peace officer's wound.

Captain (later Admiral) Farragut was at Benicia with the sloops-of-war *Vandalia* and *John Adams* but he refused to obey the governor's orders to bombard the fort. However Captain Boutwell of the *John Adams,* a personal friend of Judge Terry, took his vessel to San Francisco, assumed position at the foot of Battery Street and threatened to shell the whole neighborhood if the judge were executed. It was a tense situation while the wounded man fought with death. It was fortunate for all that he recovered. The judge served a term for assault with a deadly weapon and when discharged from prison took refuge on the *John Adams.*

In 1859 this hot-headed dignitary was back in Sacramento and as an aftermath of the election of that year, fought a duel with David Broderick, thereby killing one of California's most influential political figures. Upon the abrupt and shocking demise of Broderick, a wave of sympathetic support of his policies worked towards the success of the Republicans in the state, slanting its policy away from the pro-slavery factions. (John W. Caughey, *California,* N.Y., 1947, pp. 347-51; Cleland, *History of California.*)

time ago yet remain unanswered probably they never reached you   they were directed to Plymouth.   you know how dearly we love each other   no brotherly love is more lasting and warmer than mine although a long sixteen years have gone by since I took that dear little hand of yours in mine in an off hand boyish manner at parting at our grandmothers house   the same love is here in my bosom and time and age have had the tendency to set it deeper & firmer   write to me all about my friends and relatives, tell me about my good old grandmother & what is John & Herbert about — Caroline has she a family & have you one, and Ned Cooper what has become of him & Billy & Sammy Gleason no one writes to me   I suppose it is because I do not write to them.   it is a bad maxim scripture says if a person slaps you on one cheek turn around and slap him on the other (I beleive I have forgotten since being a Catholic) but it is some how that way.

   Kate sends any quantity of love
          Your Affectionate Brother   James

———

                              Monterey   Oct. 16th 1858
To Herbert Gleason, Plymouth
My dear Brother

   Owing to being absent from Monterey, yours of Aug 2d has not been placed in my hands untill now, and I hasten to reply, giving you thanks for your long letter.

   About the affairs of William Paty's Estate I know very little about. John has been the active Administrator in the matter and when it has been so that he could not attend to it himself he employed counsel. it has been impossible for me to give attention to it, my business keeping me here at Monterey.   for the last few years the Estate has been at a stand still for what reason I know not. I have not seen Capt Paty for more than two years but I receive letters from him now and then and am informed that the balance of the real property of the Estate has been ordered to be sold at different times and the same has been offered at public sale and no bidders owing to the property being covered with other titles &c   Capt Paty has however made arrangements to have a final settlement of the Estate by the time he arrives on the Coast again as he wrote me, which will be in about one month. I have been anxious to have the Administration closed for some time owing to my having funds locked up in the Probate Court at Oahu and cannot get it untill the Estate is settled and I cannot get any satisfactory reason why it is retained by that Court.   the simple fact of the case is this, in 1849 Paty & Co & myself invested $15000. in lumber, entrusted it to an agent to dispose of & the agent converted the money to his own use & left for the Sandwich Islands.   he was followed up and finally part of the money recovered and is now and has been for several years lying in the Probate Court at Oahu awaiting the settlement of Paty's estate.   they have no right whatever to withold my portion of the money it being about the amount of $3000 my portion as recovered. Paty's last letter tells me that Martha Ann has a counsellor by the name of Dr. Smith who will probably marry her or her daughter as appearances show and he is manageing to get all he can for Martha Ann out of the Estate and starting up old accounts to try to bring us in debt to the Estate. I expect I will have to go to the islands yet before I can get my money.   they seem to be fixing the matter to suit themselves.

About revoking the Power of Attorney to John do not do it.   he is honest and his intentions are good. I have every confidence in him that he will do all in his power for his mother towards her getting her money, but he is slow and I think he is harrassed to death by persons intermedling. If they will let him alone everything will come out right. John has my power of attorney to receive my money at the islands which proves my confidence in him.

About the notes given by John & William I do not know in whose possession they are. I supposed that the interest on them had been remitted by John and Martha Ann from time to time and that Grandmother was kept in funds. I had no other reason to think so more than John has told me in his letters that it has been difficult for him to get money to send to his mother.

When John arrives on the Coast again I will if possible go to San Francisco to see him to ascertain how matters are, and I will then write you and perhaps give you some more satisfactory information for at present I am as much in the dark about it as you are at home.

I have been sick for the last few weeks with a derangement of the liver. I am all right again now but I have lost a great deal of flesh and feel week.   as soon as I reach my usual standard of weight again I will have my likeness taken and send it. Now there is nothing of me to take except my hat and boots.

I still continue in my old office as County Clerk & Recorder, and it pays very well.   my term of office expires next October and then I think I will bid adieu to office life and take to the Country.

My family are all well and my wife who is at my side now while writing this tells me to give her love to you all. My boys and girls are growing up finely. they are all with me except my eldest boy who is at San Antonio at School.

With my best love to you all
I am your affectionate Brother   Jas H. Gleason

At Sea off California   July 20th 1859

My Dear Brother

I have been at the Sandwich Islands and now while writing I find myself within a few days sail of San Francisco. I have been absent from home since the 18th day of May the longest absence from my wife since our marriage. I left home in somewhat feeble health and now return vigorous and healthy. I have been compelled to make this trip to the islands to recover from Aunt Martha Ann the money she has had in her possession belonging to me since her return to the islands from the Eastern States. Uncle John has had my power of Attorney for the last three years to get the money & remit to me and he has repeatedly demanded the same and she refused to give the money up untill compelled to, her plea being that we as administrators had badly managed the Estate of William on the Coast and sacraficed the property, and she would finally hold us legally responsible for damages &c and for this reason she withheld my money. Now be this as it may, when we took out letters of Administration we gave bonds in the sum of $60,000 and between Paty myself and the bondsmen there is sufficient available property to satisfy any demand which might be found against us as Adm's therefore she had no right to deprive me of the use of my money for so long a time even had we badly administered upon the estate which we most emphatically deny. Uncle John has had the entire management of the estate since the first and he has done the best that he could in every instance for the benefit of the heirs, why should he not?   he had nothing to gain by delay or sacrafice of the property as they charge us with whenever any property of the estate has been sold it has been necessary to do so to meet demands against the Estate and delay in settling up the estate has been no fault of Uncle John.   the peculiar position of the real property being owned with other parties and also Martha Ann's letters to Uncle John from time to time charging him not to sell if it could be avoided, at a sacrafice has caused the delay in settling up the estate. Uncle John has acted throughout the administration of the estate of his brother William honestly and disinterestedly always with a view to do the best he could for the benefit of the heirs devoting his time and trouble and money to this object always when in doubt acting under the advice of William's intimate friends on the Coast, and for this he gains the ill will of his sister. every act that Uncle John has done as adm'r has passed the examination of the probate Court and duly approved and confirmed by the Court at San Francisco and the records show a faithful discharge of his duty. So much for Uncle John — now I'll write some about myself. I will explain first about the nature of my claim against Aunt Martha Ann.   in 1849 William & myself purchased one half of a cargo of lumber jointly with a Mr. Robertson the other half for $30,000 and the cargo was placed in the hands of the latter at Sacramento for sale and on settlement he represented that nothing was coming to us. Uncle John "smelled rat" and followed him up in San Francisco and upon an investigation into the matter it was found that he owed us $3700. for which amount he gave his notes and left for the Sandwich Islands.   the notes were collected by the Administrator of Uncle Wm's estate in 1852 and by him the money was placed out at interest at 2% per month and on Aunt Martha Ann's return to the islands the whole, principal and interest was turned over to her and up to this time she has enjoyed the interest on my money $1800. my half since 1852 seven years. On my arrival at the Islands I made a demand on Dr. Smith who is Martha Ann's agent and Nelly's future husband for my money and he refused to pay over any part of it intimating that a bill of damages would be brought against me for improper management of the estate, charging as one fact and which he harped upon most that at a time when Paty was absent to China that I sold some valuable property belonging to the estate at a great sacrafice when there was no necessity to sell. Now this is the only action I took in the whole management of the estate and I was obliged to act owing to Capt Paty's absence. The Adm's were sued in the District Court at San Francisco for a note of Uncle Wm's that had become due & interest & there being no money on hand a sale had to be made of some property to meet the note otherwise a judgement and execution would have issued out of the District Court against us as Administrators. Therefore it was better to have a sale of the property by order of the Probate Court which was done and in the meantime we were granted a stay of proceedings in the District Court for a certain time so as to enable us to sell at better advantage.

It seems that Dr. Smith was entirely ignorant of these facts consequently he had a perfect right to talk about law, responsibility, damages &c which he now feels sorry for after a settlement has been had & matters understood. I felt so aggregated at Dr. Smith's remarks that I had but little to say to him and I did not want to commence a lawsuit with Aunt Martha Ann if it could possibly be avoided. We finally consented on all sides to submit the whole matter to arbitration.   the most difficult part of the drama was the settlement of Paty & Co's affairs. Dr. Smith's account which he drew from the Books, made John Paty indebted to the estate as a partner of Paty & Co about $3000. whereas John Paty's account showed an amount due him from the Estate as a partner of Paty & Co & as Administrator of about $7000. When the accounts were made out & ready to be submitted for arbitration Dr. Smith examined them and he soon became convinced that Capt Paty's accounts were right and just and desired to compromise the matter before it went into arbitration, and we finally came to terms as follows. Aunt Martha Ann gave up a note which she held against Uncle John for $2300. and paid him $900. in cash and Uncle John pays me 1500.$ the note was given on account of purchase of a house in Oahu. had the matter gone before the arbitrators there is not the least doubt but that a heavy judgement would have been awarded in our favor. It has cost me about $500. in lawyers fees, passage &c to get this $1500. so I am returning home with only $1000. when I am justly and equitably entitled to $1800. principal, and two per cent interest on the same for seven years, this interest Aunt Martha Ann has actually received. Now all matters being settled and acquittances given on all sides I have not from the first and do not now entertain any unfriendly feelings towards Aunt Martha Ann. I am pleased to know that by using my money she has been greatly benefited but at the same time I could easily forgive and forget all and be perfectly reconciled had she before I left the islands acknowledged to me her indebtedness and expressed some gratitude during my stay at the islands. I was a frequent visitor at her house and in our conversations she never once alluded to business matters between ourselves her silence leads me to believe that she suffers under a guilty conscience and ashamed to avow that she has wronged me. Dr. Smith's threatening language towards me was a matter of course endorsed by her. the idea of recovering damages from us as Administrators was perfectly absurd and the point was raised by them for the purpose of an excuse to hold and enjoy the benefit of my money as long as they could and perhaps frighten me into a compromise. I never would have compromised the matter in the world had my claim been against any other person but a relative. If Smith thought they had any claim against us they would have pushed it through to the last dollar. when they retained a lawyer I looked forward to an endless and expensive lawsuit, lawyers will always get their clients into trouble anyhow if they can get a fee, but fortunately they found an honest man and I suppose he advised them to get out of it the best way they could by compromise which was effected finally as I have before stated.

Aunt Martha Ann is very bitter towards Uncle John. she does him a great wrong in speaking and writing so much against him. Uncle John's character for honesty and integrity however stands to high and firm to be shaken in the least by anything she or anyone else can say against him.

I am now on the last page and must close. Uncle John is writing home by this mail and I suppose he will give you a perfect history of affairs I have stated what has transpired during my stay at the islands and I have written impartially and stated what can be relied upon as true facts.

I had been absent from the islands fourteen years and I anticipated a pleasant time with my old friends, but I had to tend to work from the first day I arrived untill the day we sailed in assisting Uncle John in the old Paty & Co accounts so as to affect a settlement they refused to settle with me untill a settlement was had with Uncle John   they expected to get enough out of him to pay me but they were sadly disappointed in the end, and I suppose they give me no thanks for ferreting out the errors in their a/cs and making out Uncle John's a/cs in their proper shape.

July 25th — We arrv'd yesterday and I hear my family are all well I leave soon for Monterey. Give my love to all the folks at home Grandmother in particular. I hope her health is better, how I long to see her.

Your aff't Brother   Jas H. Gleason

Finis

The letters of James Henry Gleason end here, likely due to failing strength, for he was a frail man in spite of his assertions that he was in good health most of the time. Mr. Gleason died at Monterey in 1861 at the age of thirty-eight years and was buried beneath the pines in the Monterey cemetery.

Appendix I

TRIBUTE TO JAMES HENRY GLEASON
by *William Heath Davis (1899)*

Among the names of the American pioneers of California, whose lives shaped the destiny and adorned the history of the state, none are more deserving of favorable mention than that of James H. Gleason. Descended from an old and respectable family of Massachusetts, he was born at Plymouth in that State, October 22nd 1823, and there he passed his childhood, and received a liberal and accomplished education in Boston, looking forward however more to a business, than a professional or a literary career, in either of which he was well adapted by nature to excel.

Boston, the cradle of American liberty, and the foster mother of American art, letters, science, and enterprise! Here amid all the classic and historic traditions that cluster around the place of his birth and young manhood, the mind of young Gleason was imbued with that intense Americanism that so notably characterized his whole life. At eight years of age he lost his mother, whom he deeply loved, which event made a lasting impression upon his refined and sensitive nature. In 1841, Mr. Gleason bid a final farewell to his native home and embarked for Honolulu on the Sandwich Islands, in the noted old ship "California." The years 1842, 1843 and 1844, Mr. Gleason remained principally at Honolulu, attending to the business of his Uncle, Captain John Paty, in the capacity of agent, clerk, bookkeeper &c — making however several trips to this coast, in which he visited all the seaports from

San Blas in the South to Sitka of the north; in all which he was noted for his intelligent observation, strict fidelity, good judgement and careful attention to business. In fact he was always remarkable for his unaffected honesty, pleasing manners, and the faithful performance of every trust confided to his care. In 1845 he came to Monterey, then the Capital of "all of the Californias," and there in this beautiful and historical old town he permanently resided until the time of his death, which occurred in the year 1861. From his first advent into Monterey until after the final acquisition of the country by the Americans, Mr. Gleason was engaged in Mercantile pursuits, but took an active and intelligent interest in all the exciting events that finally resulted in the annexation of the country to the American republic, a consummation he anxiously hoped for and ardently favored. Being a leading and influential citizen when the American naval and military forces occupied Monterey he greatly aided and assisted the officials by the exercise of his sound judgement, and wise Counsel. When the starry banner of his much loved native land was unfurled over the Old Capitol building in Monterey his heart thrilled with joy, and delight, and patriotic pride. He did much to make the society of Monterey pleasant and agreeable to all, and to reconcile the Spanish population to the new order of things, for his fairness and high sense of justice was recognized by every one. Upon the adoption of the Constitution and the organization of the state government Mr. Gleason became connected with the office of County Clerk and Recorder of Monterey County, with which, as either chief clerk or deputy, he remained until his failing health compelled him to retire from the exercise of all official or public duties, which he did a short time before his death; but whether as chief or deputy he always had the supervision and entire control of the office, the duties of which he performed with marked ability, scrupulous fidelity and unquestioned honesty.

Mr. Gleason was not in the ordinary sense of that term a politician yet he entertained very decided political opinions, and these opinions were in accord with the primal principles and doctrines of the old Republican party, and early in 1856 he became an avowed adherent of that great National party. At that time there were but two others in the County, one of whom was George Chalmers, then and yet, living in the town of San Juan. These three men commenced an active and aggressive campaign, and by circulating republican literature, in both the English and the Spanish languages, and incessant and effective speech making, they only lacked a few votes of carrying the county for Fremont and Dayton at the presidential election. Notwithstanding his party was then in a hopeless minority Mr. Gleason was elected in 1857 to the office of County Clerk and Recorder by a large majority, which tends to show his great personal popularity with the people of his County. In fact he was one of those fortunate men of whom it may be truly said "he never had an enemy." He lived to see the inauguration of Mr. Lincoln as President of the United States, and the commencement of his administration in a time of turbulence and civil war, but to the very last he lost none of his sublime faith in the ultimate triumph of human freedom, the unity of the American people and the honor and glory of the American name, and American Nationality. Mr. Gleason was somewhat below the medium size, handsome in person, of affable and pleasing manners, and possessed a genial wit, and a refined sense of humor that rendered his company and conversation positively charming. Besides his wife, who was noted for her beauty, as well as for every attribute of goodness that adorns a woman, he left four sons, and four daughters. The daughters are all married, and yet living here in California, but the sons have all departed this life. Of his name, however there are three grandchildren residing here in Los Angeles, James Henry Gleason and Joe Duncan Gleason, both youths of much intelligence and bright minds, who give great promise of a useful manhood, and Miss Pearl Gleason who is well known as a musician, elocutionist and young lady of literary attainments. Mr. Gleason died respected, honored and lamented by all who knew him, and this is written as an affectionate tribute to his memory, for he was a loved and cherished friend during my earlier and my better days. He now sleeps beneath the cypress and the pine, in the Monterey cemetery on the shore of that beautiful bay where the waters of the broad Pacific sing an everlasting requiem to his departed soul.

Wm H. Davis

Appendix II

WILLIAM HEATH DAVIS
  by Duncan Gleason

William Heath Davis, eye witness to the events of the 1840s and '50s, as was James Henry Gleason, came to California in 1838 aboard the bark "Don Quixote" and later served for a time as her supercargo.

While visiting at our home in Los Angeles, Mr. Davis wrote the preceding recollections of James Henry Gleason at the request of my mother, who contemplated arranging the Gleason letters for publication. She, in turn, supplied much information for Mr. Davis' proposed book "Seventy-Five Years in California."

As a boy of sixteen, I was doing art work for a local engraving house and Mr. Davis had me make some pen and ink illustrations for his book, which was to be an enlargement of his "Sixty Years in California." The manuscript and illustrations were in his office in the Montgomery Block but during the San Francisco fire of 1906, although the building was not destroyed, the material was stolen. Mr. Davis died at Hayward, California, in April of 1909, at the age of eighty-seven years.

J Duncan Gleason

Index

Acapulco: 91
Admittance (vessel): 93
Aguardiente (brandy): 136
Alert (vessel): 19, 93
Alligator (vessel): 139
Alta California (newspaper): 133
Alvarado, Juan Bautista: 44; joins Castro, 115; home, illus., 120
Angola (vessel): 89-90, 98, 99, 110, 112
Anthous, I: of Honolulu, 70
Apollo (vessel): 99
Argüello, Santiago: 140
Armstrong, Capt. James: 45
Armstrong, Rev. Mr: 81
Artemise (vessel): 59

Baker, Capt: 190
Ballast Point (San Diego): 139
Baltimore (vessel): 192
Bandini, Juan: 108, 140, 157
Bandini, Mrs. Juan (Dolores Estudillo): 157
Barnes, George: 169, 175
Barnes, Mrs. I: 92
Barnes, Mrs. Southard: 92
Barnstable (vessel): 98, 127, 152, 155
Bartholomew Gosnold (vessel): 60
Bartlett, Washington A: alcalde at Yerba Buena, 122
Beale, Lt. Edwin: 122
Bear Flag: raised, 104, 111; illus., 117
Behering (vessel): *see Bhering*
Beldin, Josiah: letter to Gleason, 104; letters from Gleason, 95, 96, 98, 127-29; in San Francisco, 131; mentioned, 93, 94, 102, 139
Benecia (vessel): 203

Benicia: Gleason property, 153, 168
Bernice (Hawaiian princess): 78, 79
Bhering (vessel): 55, 58, 63, 66, 67, 71, 72
Boardman, Mr: in Sandwich Islands, 114, 134
Bolivar (vessel): 36
Boston (vessel): 51, 53-55
Bourne, Jonathan: buys *Lagoda,* 133
Bourne Memorial Museum (Mass.): 133
Boutwell, Capt: of *John Adams,* 203
Brandywine (vessel): 78
Brannan, Samuel: mentioned, 133, 171, 202; deed to Gleason, illus., 138
Brewer, Capt: 35, 55; wife, 36
Brewer, C. & Co: in Oahu, 123
Briganza (vessel): 33, 34
Broderick, David: 203
Brooklyn (vessel): 133, 135, 136, 171
Brown, John (Juan Flaco): 140
Bryant & Sturgis Co: 19; owners of vessel *Admittance,* 93-94
Bull (vessel): 84

California (state): mineral wealth, 108-10
California (vessel): 19, 20, 22, 42, 169, 213
California Battalion: 139
California Star (newspaper): 133
Californian (newspaper): 132, 133
Californians: under Castro, 114-16
Cape Blanco (Patagonia): 21
Cape Horn: 21, 22
Cape St. Johns (Staten Land): 22
Cape San Lucas (Lower Calif.): 123, 124

Carrillo, José Antonio: 115, 116
Carson, Kit: 122
Carter, Capt: 55
Carver, Capt. William: 82, 84
Carysfort (vessel): 51, 59, 60
Casey, James P: 202
Cash, Capt: of vessel *George*, 46
Castillero, Andrés: 94; discovers quicksilver mine, 109
Castro, José: at Sonoma, 94, 103, 104; proclamations, 106-08; at Santa Clara, 111; in Monterey, 112, 113; heads Californians, 115-16; Frémont seeks, 127, 131, 132, 139; in Mexico, 140
Catalina Island: silver mines, 109
Chacabuca (vessel): 30
Chalmers, George: 215
Chenamus (vessel): 42, 44, 46, 47, 87
Clark, Capt: of *Miceno*, 57
Cockroaches: problem with, 68-69
Cole, Thomas: 96
Coleman, William T: 202
Collingwood (vessel): 116; in Mexico, 123, 124
Colton, Walter: 132
Columbia (vessel): 105
Congo (vessel): 20
Congress (vessel): 45, 74, 87, 93, 97, 123, 139
Constellation (vessel): 60-62, 64, 65
Constitution (vessel): 64
Cooper, J.B: 144
Cooper, Ned: 204
Cora, Charles: 202
Cummins, Mr: of the *Bhering*, 72, 81
Cyane (vessel): 44, 63, 66, 68, 70; in Monterey, 96-97, 112, 114, 116; in San Diego, 126, 139; captures *Malek Adhel*, 154

Dale (vessel): 141
Dallas, Commodore: 45, 67, 70
Damon, S.C: 67
Dana, Richard Henry, Jr: 19
Davis, John C: 96
Davis, R.G: letter from Gleason, 110-12

Davis, William Heath, Jr: in San Pedro, 110; biog. sketch, 130, 217; mentioned, 44, 45, 95, 96, 101, 158; tribute to James Henry Gleason, 213-16
Davis, Mrs. William Heath, Jr. (María de Jesús Estudillo): 44
Davis, William Heath, Sr: 130
Dead Man's Island (San Pedro): 140-41
Decatur, John P: duelist, 69-70
Delaware (vessel): 30, 33, 47, 56, 58, 61
Dike, Capt: 86-87, 88
Domínguez Rancho: 140
Dominis, Capt: 61; wife, 61, 64, 70
Don Quixote (vessel): in Oahu, 26, 34, 55, 88, 141, 145, 146, 148, 217; in Monterey, 45, 48; in Mazatlan, 124; in San Pedro, 128-130, 136; racing record, 93-94, 95; illus., 39
Doten, James: 163
Dublin (vessel): 60, 62, 64
Duel: in Sandwich Islands, 69-70
Dunn, Mr: mate on *Fama*, 90-91
duPont, Samuel: commands *Congress*, 139

Earthquakes: at Acapulco, 91-92
Easterbrooks, Capt: of vessel *Glouchester*, 29
Empire City Line: shipping in Calif., 174, 184
England: flag raised over Sandwich Islands, 54, 57
Erie (vessel): 67, 68, 69
Escamilla, Joaquín S: alcalde, Monterey, 107-08
Escamilla, Mariana: *see* Watson, Mrs.
Estrada, Adelaida: *see* Spence, D.
Estrada, José: 94
Estrada, Mariano: 144
Estudillo, Dolores: *see* Bandini, Mrs.
Estudillo, José Joaquín: 44, 130
Estudillo, María de Jesús: *see* Davis, Mrs. W.H., Jr.
Euphemia (vessel): in San Fran-

Index

cisco, 95-102, 122, 123, 127; at San Pedro, 105; in Sandwich Islands, 130, 133, 134; illus., 99

Fama (vessel): loss of, 90
Farragut, Capt: 203
Fauntleroy, Daingerfield: purser on *Savannah*, 121
Fort Gunnybags (San Francisco): 203
Fort Point (San Francisco): 112
France: takes Tahiti, Society Is., 56
Frémont, John Charles: in Calif., 111-13; in Monterey, 121, 140; at San Diego, 126; seeks Castro, 127; on *Cyane*, 139

Gansevort, Stanwood: duelist, 69
Geddes, Paul: *see* Green, T.H.
George (vessel): 46
Gillespie, Archibald H: with Frémont, 113; warns Kearny, 122; on *Cyane*, 139; in Los Angeles, 140; mentioned, 112
Gleason & Co: in Monterey, 165
Gleason, Billy: 204
Gleason, Caroline: mentioned, 165, 170, 177
Gleason, Catarina: *see* Gleason, Mrs. James H.
Gleason, Duncan: *see* Gleason, Joe
Gleason, Edward: mentioned, 72, 85, 86, 143, 155, 165, 183
Gleason, Eleanor Duncan: mother of Duncan G., 16; portrait, 28
Gleason, Father: letter from son James H., 170-71; mention, 165
Gleason, Francs A: letters from brother James H., 25-91, 124-66, 168-70, 172-98; letter from Mary Ann Paty, 91-92; portrait, 27; *see also* Tribble, Mrs. Augustus M.
Gleason, Francisca (Fanny): daughter of James H., 198-99
Gleason, Henry (Henrique; son of James H.; father of Duncan): birth, 182; mentioned, 185, 188-89, 191, 193, 199

Gleason, Herbert (brother of James H.): letters from James Henry Gleason, 167-68, 204-12; 143, 147, 152, 155, 164, 165, 175, 177, 183, 186, 188
Gleason, James Henry: letters to J. Beldin, 95, 96, 98, 127-29; letter to Robert G. Davis, 110-12; letter to father, 170-71; letters to Frances A. Gleason, 25-91, 124-66, 168-70, 172-198; to Frances Tribble, 199-204; letters to Herbert Gleason, 167-68, 204-06, 206-12; letters to Capt. John Paty, 96-97, 127; letters to William Paty, 93-95, 98-105, 112-14, 116-23, 135-36, 139; letter to Capt. Richardson, 135; letter to R. C. Wyllie, 114-16; illus. of letters, 137, 179; leaves Boston, 19; auction work, 84; in Monterey, store, 89, 151, 158; gift of gold to Frances, 164; marriage, 164-65; alderman, 177; San Francisco property, 124, 142; agent for Paty & Co., 141, 144-45, 213, 214; financial losses, 182, 185; County Clerk, 206, 214, 215; supercargo on *Malek Adhel*, 154; jury duty, 158; in San Blas, 162; in San Pedro, 95; demise, 212; tribute to, 213-16; mentioned, 217; children, 182, 185, 188-89, 191, 193-94, 198-99, 206, 216
Gleason, Mrs. James H. (María Catarina Demetria Watson; Catalina or Kate): marriage, 164-65; in San Francisco, 171; son (Henry) born, 182; garden, 186; daughter (Lucia) born, 188-89; smallpox epidemic, 193-94; daughter (Francisca) born, 195, 198; fifth child mentioned, 199; *see also* Watson, María Catarina Demetria
Gleason, James Henry (grandson of James H.): 216
Gleason, Joe Duncan (grandson of James H.): mentioned, 13, 16, 216; biog. sketch of Wm. H. Davis, Jr., 217

Gleason, John (brother of James H.): mentioned, 143, 147, 152, 155, 164, 165, 175, 177, 183, 185, 186, 188, 204
Gleason, Lucia (Lucy; daughter of James H.): birth, 188; smallpox, 193-94; mentioned, 189, 191, 199
Gleason, Marianita (daughter of James H.): 199
Gleason, Pearl (granddaughter of James H.): 216
Gleason, Samuel (Sammell, Samuell, Sammy): 152, 155, 183, 204
Gleason, William: 155
Gleason, William B: 152, 165
Gleason Street (Monterey): 146
Globe (vessel): 77
Glouchester (vessel): 29
Gold Rush: described, 159-61
Golden State (vessel): 189
Gonsales, José Rafael: 108
Great Britain: demands on Hawaii, 51-54
Green, Talbot H. (Paul Geddes known as in Calif.): Collector of Port, Monterey, 131, 143, 146, 171; mentioned, 185
Gregg and Company (Monterey): 144
Grimes, Hiram and Eliab: purchase *Euphemia*, 101

Haalilio: 59; funeral for, 81-82
Hall, I.T: 35, 165
Hamsley, Lt: of the *Levant*, 126
Hartnell, William: of Monterey, 114, 200
Hawaii: *see* Sandwich Is.
Hawaiian flag: illus., 49
Hazard (vessel): 60, 61, 64
Hencley, Lt: of the *Collingwood*, 116, 123
Hinckley (Hinkley) William Sturgis: death, 114
Holmes, Capt. John: 45
Holmes, Oliver: daughter marries Wm. H. Davis, Jr., 130
Holmes, Rachel: *see* Larkin, Mrs. T.

Honolulu: 29; Wm. Paty Collector of Customs, 65-66; mentioned, 213
Honolulu (vessel): 152
Hooper, William: Amer. consul, 52; wife's party, 65
Howard, William D.M: 19, marriage, 20
Howard, Mrs. W.D.M. (Mary Warren): 20
Hudson's Bay Company: 105
Hull, Capt: of U.S. *Warren*, 154

Ide, William B: revolt and proclamation, 103-06, 111, 113, 115
Independence (vessel): 142
Inez (vessel): 78, 80
Insurgente (vessel): 64

Jarves, J.J: 152
John Adams (vessel): 203
Johnson, Gov. J.N: 202-03
Johnston, Capt. A.R: killed at San Pasqual, 122
Jones, George: chaplain of *Brandywine*, 78
Jones, Thomas ap Catesby: in Los Angeles, 45; Monterey debacle, 67; mentioned, 44, 141
Joseph Peabody (vessel): 36
Joven Guipuzcoana (vessel): 44, 45
Juanita (vessel): 114
Julia (vessel): 52, 203
Juno (vessel): 116

Kamehameha III: conflict with British, 52-59; flag raised, 60; victory ball, 62-63
Kamehameha III (vessel): 97
Kearny, Stephen W: 122
Kemble, Edward: buys newspaper, 133
Keoni Ana (vessel): 133
Kern, Edward: 111-12
King, James: murdered, 202
Klamath Indians: attack, 112
Knox, Mr: mate on *Bhering*, 67
Knox, Capt: on *Inez*, 77, 80
Kooser, Benjamin P: printer, 132

Index

L. C. Richmond (vessel) : 24
Lagoda (vessel) : 132, 133
LaPlace, Capt: of *Artemise,* 59
Larkin, Thomas Oliver: letter on mineral wealth, 108-11; purchases cargo, 102-03; revolution report, 103; prisoner, 113-14; in Boston, 175; mentioned, 45, 95, 101, 111
Larkin, Mrs. Thomas Oliver (Rachel Holmes) : 45
Leese, Jacob Primer (Leace): prisoner, 103, 111, 115; mentioned, 107
Leidesdorff, William A: report to Larkin, 103
Levant (vessel) : 114, 116, 126, 142
Long, Capt. I.C: of *Boston,* 51, 53-54
Loo Choo (vessel) : 149
Loring, E.T, & Company: 57
Loriot (vessel) : 158
Los Angeles: pueblo, 139, 140, 152
Louisa (vessel) : 45

McKinley (of Paty & Co.) : in Mazatlan, 102; in San Pedro, 131; mentioned, 136
Maddox, Lt: in San Diego, 140
Malek Adhel (vessel) : 154, 158
Mansion House (Honolulu) : 64, 69, 70
Manuokawai (vessel) : 100
Marshall, James: discovers gold, 159
Marshall, W.S: murder, 202
Mary Ann (vessel) : 154
Mary Frances (vessel) : 162
Maui (Mowe) : 24
Mazatlan (Mexico): *Don Quixote* at, 89, 124; Paty at, 102; Sloat at, 121; *Warren* at, 154
Mellus, Howard & Company: 20
Merrimac (vessel) : 74
Mervine, William: of *Cyane,* 97, 121, 136, 140
Mexico: rumors of war, 90, 91; war declared, 121-22, 131
Miceno (vessel) : 57
Micheltorena, Manuel: 45
Mindoro (vessel) : 85, 87
Mineral wealth: of Calif., 108-10

Monterey: Jones in, 44; business, 97; American flag over, 101; Gov. Alvarado's home, illus., 120; port of, 131; Gleason land holdings, 146; customhouse illus., 119
Montgomery, Capt: of *Portsmouth,* 116; takes Yerba Buena, 122
Montreal (vessel) : 80, 81
Moore, Capt: killed in battle, 122
Mormons: counterfeit coin case, 158; in gold fields, 159
Moscow (vessel) : 110, 112, 127
"Mule Hill": battle at, 122

Nelly Blue: *see* Paty, Hellen D.
New Helvetia (Calif.) : 159
Newcastle (vessel) : 45
Nimrod (vessel) : 73
Northern (vessel) : 185
Nuuanu Valley: on Oahu, 63, 65
Nye, Capt. Gorman H: of *Bolivar,* 36; wife, 36; of *Fama,* 90, 91; on *Euphemia,* 123; mentioned, 105, 114

Oahu: *see* Sandwich Is.
Olga (vessel) : 155
Oregon (vessel) : 169, 181
Osio, Antonio: 97
Osio, Nacisa de: 153
Owyhee: *see* Sandwich Is.

Pacific Mail Steamship Co: 169
Pacific Squadron: 141
Page, Commodore: commands *Levant,* 126
Panama (vessel) : 163, 169
Parker House (San Francisco) : in ruins, 187
Paty, Caroline Frances: cousin of Gleason, death, 76
Paty, Hellen D. (Nelly Blue): mentioned, 31, 34, 44, 49, 56, 61, 71, 76, 88, 209
Paty, John (son of Wm.) : 205-06
Paty, Capt. John (uncle of Gleason): letters from James Henry Gleason, 96-97, 127; in Mazatlan, 101, 102;

Paty, Capt. John (contin.)
business problems, 136, 141; co-owner of *Malek Adhel*, 154; in Sandwich Islands, 174; in Monterey, 176; San Francisco, 187, 192; in China, 190, 191; manages Paty estate, 204-05, 207-12; portrait, 37; log book, illus., 100; mentioned, 29, 31, 39, 45, 57, 72, 86-88, 92, 93, 114, 130, 131, 149
Paty, Mrs. John (Mary Ann): letter to Frances A. Gleason, 91-92; on *Don Quixote*, 35, 126, 135; in Monterey, 45; in Oahu, 55; children, 56-58, 147; mentioned, 26, 29, 31, 32
Paty, John Henry (son of Capt. John): on *Don Quixote*, 35; mentioned, 31, 55, 61, 71, 88, 192
Paty, Thomas (uncle of Gleason): 92
Paty, William (uncle of Gleason): letters from James Henry Gleason, 93-95, 98-105, 112-114, 116-23, 130-36, 139; new home, 34; illness, 42; success, 65; in Oahu, 57, 95, 161; copy of Larkin's letter sent to, 108-10; problems with estate, 173, 174, 189, 204-05, 207-12; mentioned, 29, 32, 35, 43
Paty, William, Jr. (son of William): 88
Paty, Mrs. William (Martha Ann): returned to U.S., 173, 175, 177, 183, 186, 187; estate problems, 205-12; mentioned, 26, 29, 34, 43, 58
Paty & Co: business, 95, 148, debts, 151, 154; sell *Malek Adhel*, 158; financial problems, 208-11
Paulet, Lord George T: threats, 51-52; visits Kamehameha, 53-54; possesses Sandwich Is., 57, 59, 61
Penhallow, Capt. David P: 69
Phelps, Capt. William D: 112; co-owner of *Malek Adhel*, 154
Pico, Andrés: 122
Pico, Pío: governor, 94; joins Castro, 139; in Mexico, 140

Pilgrim (vessel): 19
Pizarro (vessel): 144
Point Pinos: 184
Poor, Mr: of the *Erie*, 68
Portsmouth (vessel): 101, 113, 116, 122
Portsmouth Square (San Francisco): 122, 142
Prebble (vessel): 143
Prudon, Victor: prisoner, 103, 107, 111, 115

Ramage Press: 132, 133
Regulator (vessel): 154
Reynolds Wharf (Oahu): 52, 53
Richards, Rev. William: 59
Richardson, Capt. (of the *Brooklyn*): letter from Gleason, 135; mentioned, 109
Richardson, Mr: 116
Richardson, William: assassinated, 202
Rico, Francisco: 115
Rio Packet (vessel): 20
Robertson, Mr: buys lumber, 208
Robinson, Mr: of the *Erie*, 68
Robinson, Mr: clerk of *Moscow*, 110
Rogers, Capt: of *Wm. & Eliza*, 71
Roney, Midshipman: of *Cyane*, 70
Rover (vessel): 90
Rowan, Lt: in San Diego, 140
Russell, Capt: of *Bartholomew Gosnold*, 60

Sacramento: unrest in, 103; flooded, 191; fire, 192; mentioned, 167, 168
San Antonio, Mission of: 144
San Benito Rancho: 195
San Blas (Mexico): 162
San Carlos, Mission of: 144
San Diego: 140
San Francisco: 122, 130; ships listed at, 127, 142; compared to Monterey, 172-73; fire, 187; Vigilance Committee, 200-04; (1906) fire, 217
San Francisco *Bulletin* (newspaper): 202

Index

San José Pueblo: Ide's proclamation, 104; Gleason in, 168
San Juan Bautista: unrest in, 103
San Luis Obispo: 130
San Pasqual: battle at, 122
San Pedro: *Don Quixote* at, 95, 123, 128-30; *Euphemia* at, 105; John Paty at, 127; Stockton in, 142; mentioned, 109, 110, 139, 140
San Rafael: 115
Sandwich (Hawaiian) Islands: Gleason arrives at, 24; flag of, 49; Gleason in, 25-88; independence gained, 59-60; victory observed, 63-65; flag illus., 49; mentioned, 25, 26, 29, 65-66, 213
Santa Barbara: *Fama* lost near, 90; *Don Quixote* at, 130; mentioned, 139
Santa Clara: Castro headquarters, 107, 108; mentioned, 136, 139
Sarah & Abigail (vessel): 35, 36
Savannah (vessel): 114, 116, 140
Semple, Robert: 132
Sherman, Capt: of whaler *Nimrod*, 73
Sherman, Wm. T: resignation, 201; Adj.-Gen., 203
Silva, Capt. Mariana: surrenders Monterey, 45
Simpson, Alexander: British consul to Hawaii, 59
Sitka (Alaska): 102
Sloat, John D: takes Monterey, 116, 121, 124; on the *Levant*, 126; mentioned, 123, 139
Smallpox: in Monterey, 193
Smith, Dr: Martha Ann Paty's agent, 205, 209-11
Snow, Capt: of the *Bhering*, 63, 66
Society Islands: possessed by France, 56
Society of California Pioneers: 20
Sonoma: revolt at, 103-05, 111-13; Ide's proclamation and followers, 106, 115, 116
Southworth, Eli: joint owner of Gleason store, 158

Spear, Nathan: Monterey merchant, 130
Spence, David: 144; marries Adelaida Estrada, 144
Spooner, John: 169
Star (newspaper): 171
Stearns, Abel: employs W. D. M. Howard, 20
Sterling (vessel): 127, 140
Stickney, Capt: of *Wm. Gray*, 48
Stockton, Robert: 122; proclamation, 133; at San Pedro, 139, 142; in San Diego, 157
Stokes, Dr: 103, 169
Sullivan, John W: Boston merchant, 89, 124
Sutter, John: 159
Sutter's Fort: 111, 112

Tahiti: French possession, 56
Talbot, Lt: at Santa Barbara, 139
Talbot (vessel): 81, 82
Tasso (vessel): 127, 128, 129
Taylor, Edward: 92
Terry, David S: 203
Teschmacher, Henry Frederick (Teschmaker): 147-49, 175, 176
Thomas, Rear-Admiral: hoists Hawaiian ensign, 59, 60, 68, 77
Toomes, Albert G. (Tooms): 98, 129
Torre, Capt. Gabriel de la: 112
Torre, Joaquin de la: 115
Tribble, Augustus M. (A.M.T.): engaged to Frances Gleason, 152; mentioned, 41, 46, 155, 165, 170, 175
Tribble, Mrs. Augustus M. (Frances A. Gleason): letter from James Henry Gleason, 199-204; *see also* Gleason, Frances A.
Trinidad Bay (Calif.): gold at, 171

Union Hotel (San Francisco): in ruins, 187
United States (vessel): 44, 45, 47, 64, 65, 141

Vallejo, Mariano G: prisoner, 103, 107, 111, 115

Vallejo, Salvador: prisoner, 103, 107, 111, 115
Valliant (vessel): 102
Vancouver, George: 54
Vancouver (vessel): 101
Vandalia (vessel): 95, 98, 127, 140, 203
Vanguard (vessel): 44
Vargue, John: 85
Varney, Capt. Samuel: of *Angola*, 98, 102, 112
Vengeance (vessel): 64
Victoria (vessel): 35, 42
Vigilance Committee: 200-04
Vignes, Louis: 45
Vincennes (vessel): 78
Volunteer (vessel): 45
Von Pfister, Edward H. (Von Pfisher): 105

Waltz: 90
War: rumors of, 90, 91; declared, 121-22, 131
Warren (vessel): 154, 159
Watson, James (Santiago Pedro): father-in-law of Gleason, 125, 144, 164
Watson, Mrs. James (Mariana Escamilla): 144
Watson, María Catarina Demetria (Catalina, Kate): engagement to James Henry Gleason, 125, 143-45, 148-50; description of, 151, 157, 159; married, 164; *see also* Gleason, Mrs. J.H.
Watson, Thomas: son of James, 195
Wilson, Mr: on the *Cyane*, 67, 70
White, George: mentioned, 30, 32, 35, 55, 62, 73, 74, 165
William & Eliza (vessel): 71
William Gray (Grey) (vessel): 42-44, 46-48, 52, 56
Wigman, Lewis: 96
Wyllie, Robert Crichton: letter from James Henry Gleason, 114-16

Yerba Buena: 122, 130; *see also* San Francisco

Zamorano, Agustín: 132